Hypochondria

Simple Steps to Control Your Health Anxiety for Life

(How I Went Thought Health Anxiety, Social Anxiety, Depression, Hypochondria and Defeat Them All)

William Farrow

I0095444

Published By **Tyson Maxwell**

William Farrow

Hypochondria: Simple Steps to Control Your Health Anxiety for Life (How I Went Thought Health Anxiety, Social Anxiety, Depression, Hypochondria and Defeat Them All)

ISBN   978-1-998038-39-8

No part of this guidebook shall be reproduced in any form without permission in writing from the publisher except in the case of brief quotations embodied in critical articles or reviews.

Legal & Disclaimer

Upon using the information contained in this book, you agree to hold harmless the Author from and against any damages, costs, and expenses, including any legal fees potentially resulting from the application of any of the information provided by this guide. This disclaimer applies to any damages or injury caused by the use and application, whether directly or indirectly, of any advice or information presented, whether for breach of contract, tort, negligence, personal injury, criminal intent, or under any other cause of action.

You agree to accept all risks of using the information presented inside this book. You need to consult a professional medical practitioner in order to ensure you are both able and healthy enough to participate in this program.

Table Of Contents

Chapter 1: Hypochondria in Each and Every One of Us...

Whatever degree of hypochondria that you are suffering from regardless of how severe the condition has impacted your life, the advice I'd like to convey is exactly the same. There is no need to be afflicted by anxiety and depression or stricken by hypochondriac thought patterns in order for this book to be useful to you. Actually every thought you think of is not aimed at pushing your life forward and is not based on being a lover of yourself and trusting in the course of your life and any idea that does not help you to be in your most optimal state, or allow you to unlock your maximum potential, is not a good idea initially or even be a part of your head.

I have come across lots of individuals who have told me that they regularly be concerned about their well-being. The majority of them aren't influenced by their thoughts as it is not a regular thing however, it's an initial step and their time worried is a waste. It is my mantra to them that instead of worrying about the reason you're worrying over your health so much and act on it instead.

It is the acuity the book is encouraging Hypochondria is a condition that is something to be taken care of promptly and effectively, by taking a close look at different aspects of your daily life, and your role to fulfill in your life. This fear seems to me as distractions, result of in positive thoughts or a lack of motivation in living and a lack of enthusiasm and an absence of an affirming conviction system. They are an excellent justification for that you will not be capable of achieving the things you'd like to achieve as you unconsciously do think you're not capable of achieving your desires.

Your Current State

Understanding Your Pains

This paragraph is dedicated to be with you and to let you know that I truly understand your pain and do not intend to diminish the pain you feel or claiming that they're simple to resolve. I understand what I'm speaking about. It is not my intention to suggest that any other condition is more difficult than those caused by hypochondria. In the majority of cases the condition you suffer from may be more severe, since you are able to show the signs of a variety of diseases. A person with cancer may be diagnosed with cancer only, however it is manifesting symptoms of the disease and, sometimes possibly, other diseases in the same way. It is possible that you are experiencing greater pain due to "the disease you think you have" than what it would be should you have actually had the condition. It's because It's all within your head.

It is your intention to claim, "It is showing on my body too!" Well, it's a given! The body will show it as it is as long as the thought of getting sick is a part of your mind, and you accept the idea! There's nothing to be surprised about. I am sure you're in discomfort, and I am aware that your body pulls you around and exerts control over your brain. I am aware your brain can appear to be like an unrepresentative entity and that your fears appear to be generated through your body. they originate from a portion of your brain which it is not your control However, I know the things you're capable of and the ways you can get back in the control of your situation.

A Self-fueling, Self-validating Condition

If you look around your body, you'll always discover some thing. You have millions of cell within your body as well as an array of biochemical processes You are exposed constantly to a myriad of circumstances, smells, environmental as well as foreign substances and even organisms. The flatulence of the passenger that is sitting beside you in the bus, or the irritable feel of your pillowcase which has been labeled "New Materials Only "... It's true! The body is constantly subject to the environmental stress it must deal with! So it's only natural some things can be wrong. A pimple may appear from time the time, or even a tiny scratch... This is why that you're in the spotlight of your own mind I'm with you there is always some thing. It's a good start...

The process begins with an idea and a bit of doubt or an ounce of fear and then you consider the knowledge that you know about the biology of illnesses to support it. Sorry for labelling the knowledge you have as nil and yet it's when compared to science-based knowledge in addition to the variety of diseases and ailments that are currently in existence. The thought may originate from an observation or a recollection, but rather because you didn't have anything other to consider and allowed your mind to wander into the world that you are most afraid of. The thought or fear comes back frequently and, the next time you notice, it's the only thing you think about. The first thing you do is wake up and hurry to get your reflection. Instead of contemplating how great your day is likely to be, or the things you could create to make it more awesome and instead of getting up each day feeling grateful for the blessings life has bestowed to you it is a worry about the things that are going out of your body, and consequently, your potential loss in the near future. What is the most important thing you've not experienced in your life, but may result in you not receiving... Then... you know what you find that your day has become no longer awesome.

It never ceases in "what is going wrong with me." Your brain is required to associate it with a myriad of different things. Put all of it in one basket so that your anxiety gets greater and provide you with a reason to pay the fear more time and attention. Are you aware of the process? A fear of just being lost in the world would not be a concern, however the thought of losing the life you might have been the most happy, rich and influential human being in the universe is terrifying. Be aware of the chance to be the person you want to be, but just for the purpose to fuel your fear: "I could have been had I not been destined be restricted by medical issues or risk losing my life." ..."

The thoughts get overwhelming, and you are feeling a kind of burden or weight over your chest throughout the day It's as if you is never given the chance to unwind. The body gets tired, and you lose your energy. Then you become less and more absent, lacking from the little pleasures in life, and are constantly being drawn by the inner voice: "Is there something wrong with me?", "Shall I get it checked?", "Is it dangerous?", "Is it possible that I have cancer and I don't know?", " Is it possible that a silent disease is eating me alive?". The cycle never ends and you need to shout "stoooooop!" and beg your brain to quiet down. However many times medical professionals and doctors reassure that you are healthy, you always feel that there's some issue with your health and your health could be in danger.

When you are fatigued and depressed and depressed, you begin to take lesser care of your health, and you begin to lose healthy practices like eating right exercise and when you get tired, it becomes harder and harder to control those thoughts that are overpowering you. It's like fighting an unending battle which you'll end up losing since all your efforts go to creating the enemy, and nothing is left.

As you grow tired You become convinced that you aren't right, you're sick. And within a short time the brain starts working its job: you begin suffering "symptoms". "Aha! I said I was experiencing something" This is like it was if you had been just waiting for these symptoms in order to prove everyone else that you were not lying!

When you begin to experience symptoms, your brain and your attention is becoming increasingly focused on the body, and signs are usually viewed with greater subjectivity than what they really are. If you conduct the blood test, and turn away, you may not feel any pain, but when you're staring at the needle, the procedure could be extremely painful. That's how intense concentration and attention can be.

The signs and symptoms are more apparent more than ever before "It can only be due to a disease", you may believe. As you accept it the more you believe it to be real and you are living exactly in line with the reality you perceive.

There are many feelings and bodily responses you may experience, with some being worse or more painful than others. These include muscles aches, fever and rashes. and elevated blood pressure. It is not the intensity of your pain a sign of whether the symptom you are experiencing is most likely the result of a condition or it is not.

When you begin looking for illnesses online, and then you come across descriptions that describe the signs or symptoms that you are experiencing. Or, you constantly exhibit symptoms that you've studied about. The more committed your research becomes online and the greater your the knowledge necessary to prove your hypochondria. Consequently it is more difficult to be a believer in doctors and the more the threat to the hypochondria you have becomes.

Then you begin talking to your family and friends concerning your issues and then act as if they are trying to assure you. In the end, you are trying to convince them there is something happening to your body. But in reality, you're actually making yourself appear more convincing.

If you are able to talk about your fears and anxiety, the more effect it will have upon your daily life. It is a problem that nothing appears to soothe you, there is nothing that seems to help you get back to reality It's as if you believe that being sick is instilled into your DNA, brain or cells. It actually is. Therefore, I would not think you should be blamed for not trusting the medical professionals in their claims that there is nothing wrong with you. There's something greater than you, and it is keeping your from putting them into practice; something so tangible that it appears to have an existence that is it's own.

Chapter 2: The Root Cause

There may be a myriad of reasons for you to have been exhibiting this behavior, and all of them can be held responsible for. Whatever is the cause the reasons are that they've caused you to forget just how powerful you are as a person, just how impressive your immunity system is, how remarkable the capacity of your body to endure is as well as how incredible your mind's power over the body and how significant your opinions can influence the world around you as well as the environment you grow within. They've made you unkind to your body, uninformed about your physical condition as well as caused you to forget the purpose you're doing here, how inventive you are and how valuable you could make to our universe as well as society, how other people need your help, how satisfying it feels to make people feel happy and how satisfying you feel when you are focusing on your family members rather than worrying about your own needs.

The goal should not be to battle your hypochondria. instead, reclaim the principles you've forgotten and the kindness of your heart when you've done this then your hypochondria should no need to be a reason for existence and it will disappear completely by itself.

Focusing on the smoke, but not the flame, your illness isn't hypochondria, but an absence of passion it is not hypochondria, but you've forgotten the importance of service and love Your illness isn't hypochondria if you forget the wonderful capabilities you have been blessed with and your uniqueness and your illness isn't hypochondria, but a failure to appreciate all the joys life can bring and the incredible chances that are waiting for you. Your illness is not hypochondria, but the failure of you to believe in the miracles of the life you live.

Changing Your Mindset; Sticking to Principles and an Empowering System of Beliefs:

Recognising Your Rights For a Happy Life

All of us need reference points, a framework of belief that helps us build our self-esteem, which gives us the feeling at ease and doing the right thing since without these principles, life isn't always as simple and the variety of choices the world offers could be confusing. There is something we need to hold onto. There are people who become fervent over certain habits and their choices, or their beliefs, creating idols from successful individuals such as stars, athletes or politicians. Certain people set up the rules and develop habits such that they wouldn't miss a hockey game of their favorite team or ensure that they go to church each Saturday... In the event that they adhere to these rules, they are sure as if they're living according to their values and their choices for their personal identity.

Today, I want you to recognize the right of living happily, to acknowledge the importance of having a smile on your face everyday, to acknowledge your rights to pleasure and happiness as well as your rights to be at peace within and enjoy your life to the highest level. It is important to keep these rights in mind and create the habit of not that no one or nothing can hinder you from your rights and freedoms. There is no circumstance, illness, nobody and any condition, especially ones that originate from your. The only thing you can do is adhere to the rights you have and work that you can do to safeguard the rights you have. Are you able to do this?

Do you recognize your right to be heard? Are you aware that you are entitled to more than to spend a moment of your time worrying about your well-being?

You are not denied the rights you enjoy. You have the right to live a healthy life and should try the best you can to maintain a great health, but you must realize that life isn't perfect and we're not in complete control. Every day, we try our best to ensure that the outcome is in our favor but we are not able to guarantee that the outcome will be positive! How are you doing? For this situation, it should be to develop an encouraging belief system that are positive as well as a nutritious diet and an active life style, ample sleep, good social interactions as well as many other.

The goal of this article isn't to define what a healthy or ideal way of life is. You know what I mean... It is important to do the best you can and above all, you need to possess the confidence to recognize that you're not in charge of every aspect of your life. If anything occurred to you, it would be a good idea to say "Well, I did my best!"

Being constantly observing your body and pondering what might cause problems isn't performing at the highest level. Being able to live a healthy and balanced life is one of the best things that you can achieve your very best. If you are devoted towards observing yourself in the process, you're actually putting a damper in other areas of your existence that contribute to the harmony that I've just discussed.

Imagine that you had an opportunity to remain in the hospital, and to be connected to a variety of medical equipments that will continuously monitor your health and wait for any anomaly to occur Would you choose to do this? What kind of lifestyle could you live? Could this be the type of life you're trying to achieve? It is, however, exactly the way you're doing it. It is not that it's difficult to not make this mistake, but you'll try your best not to.

The hypochondria I have seen is an internal struggle for your right to live an optimum health and resistance to what can be seen as a sporadic injustice of our lives since it is not our choice to be poor, sick or suffering. It's a type of an obsession with living which takes on a very wrong shape. Just as when playing Monopoly you agree to certain rules and you must do similar with life. Life has its own system and specific rules and regulations: By living, we acknowledge the fact that life isn't without risk as well as the fact that there are numerous aspects of life that we cannot be in control of, that we're creating our world like most others do (the consequence will be an amalgamation of all the factors) Our perception will be constantly shaped through social pressure and our childhood, as well as our experiences, and the most important thing is the fact that "shit happens". "Shit happens" (I promise you that this is the best advice) Yes, but there's too much beauty. numerous successes, and numerous marvels...

Paradox: Fear of Losing Life While Not Living It

It is paradoxical that you are afraid of losing your the life you have, yet you're not actually living. This means that you are already living the things you fear most. That is to say, you're actually denying your dream of living the life you've been fighting to live. You can rest assured that the situation will not become any worse. The majority of patients with chronic illnesses are smiling and striving to make the most of what is left of their lives.

Chapter 3: You Are Stronger Than That

It is essential to discover the strength within you to take on whatever you need to enjoy life and make the most of it until it's taken of you. The most important thing to remember is that you're more powerful than any illness or sickness as well as more powerful than the limitations. When you lose one eye, it is not the end of the world eye, and if it is lost sight increase your other senses so that you are in a position to get the most from the various aspects of life that which you will be able to enjoy through the body functions that you are able to perform. It's not that you can do it all by yourself; I'm not minimizing or minimizing the challenges an illness or handicap could bring to one's daily life. What I'm saying is that, if you're unwell, the problem isn't an end, and you are able to manage it.

There are people who already have the things you worry about; possess what you've given up your life to. But, we have to ask the question: Do these people continue to be able to enjoy their lives? Are they able to live their lives comfortably? Are they still entitled to rights to be alive? I would say "Of course they do/can". Why aren't you giving you the same rights, and accepting in yourself your own abilities the same rights?

Certain people suffering from illnesses and illnesses get the best from their lives, whereas people who are healthy and well are wasting their time in various ways. Instead of living with fear try to make the most of the time you have as you take pleasure in all the bodily functions, and hope it will remain that way throughout your existence. Let nothing stop you from living your life or stop you from enjoying your life because you're stronger than this!

Your ideology should include:

As long as I'm able to walk, I'll walk!

So long as I am able to be able to see, I will!

So long as I am able to breathe, I'll be able to be able to breathe!

I will never be denied the right that I am happy.

If my mouth has been mangled I'll keep smiling and smiling inside!

I am possessed by this ability in my...

In fact, you possess this ability inside your...

If you are suffering from headaches but are able to watch movies or read a great book, then take a break and watch a film or take a break to read. If you suffer from stomach cramp, but you be a good parent, then do it instead of stressing about the issue! Speak to your family: "if life ever sends me a burden I will have the strength in me to live with it, and the belief that one day it could be resolved"

The Body Is Stronger Than You Think

The body is more powerful than you believe It has a myriad of little-known instances of the rapid resolution of life-threatening illnesses. Your immune system is constantly combating numerous invaders and does a fantastic job. Your body is equipped with a variety of mechanisms for self-healing. The scarring of wounds is a simple example.

Take note of the strength and efficacy that your body (and your immune body) then let the system carry out the job it was designed to do!

If our body was this fragile, the human body is not possible. Did you realize what a miserable situation are for people living in some of the most impoverished countries of the world? There is certainly sickness and certainly there's disease, but also there's the possibility of life. Life flows everywhere.

You can search on Google, "the dirtiest man on earth". The man didn't shower throughout his life. (I am not imagining the smell). ...). Imagine the strains that the world continuously exposes him to, and how weak his immune system could be. However, he is doing well... This shows how resilient and strong the human body can be! Many parts of the globe, there are conditions out of your reach regarding the amount of dirt and harm to the human body. However, within these areas in the world, humans survive and the population is expanding. Human bodies are robust...

Most Diseases Are Not As Bad As You Imagine Them to Be

Yes there are some terrible diseases out there, but with the progress of science and the medical/pharmaceutical field most diseases are controllable and the pain and symptoms are controllable if not curable.

Face Your Fears

A good attitude is not to be scared of this illness but rather to recognize that, even if you were to suffer from something you're afraid of that you might still possess plenty of opportunity to experience and enjoy the numerous blessings life can give. What you are thinking that you are suffering from isn't preventing the book from being read It will not stop you from reading others amazing books, and also benefit from the amazing experiences that the other readers have to offer as well...

Are the ailment you believe that you suffer from preventing you from running? No? You can take a stroll through the neighborhood you love or visit a nearby park. Do you feel it is preventing you from enjoying the splendor of a blooming cherry tree? Do you have a hard time having a relationship with others and feeling loved? Are you preventing yourself from enjoying a delicious food? Are you preventing yourself from having fun listening to great music (Avoid the music "This is Why I Am Hot")? Do you have trouble enjoying a laugh? Do you have a problem making contact with a friend? Are you unable to dancing? Do you have trouble taking in the natural beauty? Are you preventing yourself from taking on a new challenge? Do you have trouble singing? Do you know if you have the illness? This isn't the end of the world as life goes on until your final breath, and I am aware, you're breathing.

There will always be the need to engage in something you enjoy Your final function is your ability to Imagine and break free from the boundaries of your physical by daydreaming, visualization, imagination and meditation.

Chapter 4: Do Not Pity Yourself

Any burden or hurdle that the world throws your way, do not make the mistake of praising yourself. Doing so will place you in a position that would rob you every ability to defeat and overcome any challenge that you're facing.

Do not feel guilty about your life because when you live in the world, you are acquiescing to the laws of the world, and you recognize that you're not in charge of anything that occurs to you, but you accept it is your responsibility to take whatever action is within your power to be at the best you can and try your best. Your worth is much more than just pity.

It is crucial that you maintain your moral high ground as well as positive outlook. Pitying yourself means admitting defeat and acknowledging weaknesses. Every single cell of your body, every one function, is affected by the situation you're at: If you imagine that you are alive, you'll pump blood into your veins. However, If you imagine disease and death, you'll put poison in the veins of your body. There is a problem that causes you to believe you're a victim of some serious ailments, however the reality is that the majority of instances, you're the not the victim, you are only a victim of your brain. situation, I have to admit it could be frustrating and limiting however it's not impossible to solve therefore there's no reason to feel sorry for yourself.

Stop Thinking That Life Is Acting Against You

Do you believe that your life is on the verge of changing towards you? If you believe your life has been sending you the diseases you're suffering from? And why aren't you unable to recognize the splendor that life exposes us every single day? Certain realities that you may think are very challenging to handle and accept, but there is no obligation to contemplate this truth until you're actually being a victim of it. In reality, the only thought you're allowed to think about a difficult scenario is being aware that you're living it, if. If you've not been diagnosed medically with any illness, and are in fact suffering, then the truth is that you're not! It's like "innocent until proven guilty" but not the other the other way around. Your health is good until you're proven that you are sick.

If you're like me I'm certain you've become a pro of imagining yourself in impossible scenarios. At first, you think you're suffering from disease A. Then one morning you realize that there's an actual cure for the disease A. You begin to think about what would happen is the possibility of me having an aversion to treatment?

Here is the place I'm going to ask: what's the reason?

You think that you're this amazing feat of science? This one of a million cases of whose condition is not discovered by a test, or has a resistance to treatment. It's only the thought of a fantasy fact, not reality that's causing you harm. The thing that harms you isn't the actual situation rather the thoughts of an experience you'd prefer not to be in. There is a freedom to consider it and If you're the an innocent victim of an obsessive thinking (I refer to this as an intrusive thinking) You have the power to reshape the thought.

The world isn't this unjust system which is threatening you, and that's giving you the most rare diseases. If you think it's an issue, you're not fair and not in line with the stats of the real world. The diseases that cause them do happen, however they're not the norm, they are an

32

exception. If I told you to purchase daily a lottery ticket and you refused, then why would you. It would be an unnecessary expense, since the odds of winning aren't that high. This is a worthwhile attempt, but not much more. However, if this rare condition were to be a prize in a lottery the worry is like if you bought daily a lottery ticket.

People who are most successful are those who have mastered the things you like to do, but also considering the ideal outcomes and luck. Are you able to do this? Do you really need to believe that you might be one of the most fortunate people in the world? You can do continue to do so until you're proved wrong. In the event that you are for the day you're proven wrong. you're too to be living your life; working on the things that you love most, all the time sending affection to those you love about, too busy helping others in greater in need than you.

You Are Here to Serve

Do you understand why you're suffering from the hypochondriasis and spend all day worrying over your health? The reason is that you've neglected to think about the purpose of your life; it can be because you often forget that you're in this to serve others, and frequently forget the satisfying and joy of doing so. Take a moment to think about your last time helping somebody else; what did it feel seeing the person's appreciation and the smile that you placed on their face. Instead of stressing that you appear less attractive than normal and you are more likely to look at ways you could improve your own happiness and make the people surrounding you more content. No matter what your title or abilities, you'll always be able to demonstrate an expert or talent that you could offer to others. Have you ever considered what you could do to get the most benefit from your expertise? Have you considered about the impact that your actions and decisions could have on the lives of other people?

When you serve others, you're making them feel on the same scale as. There is no longer a place for you to be at being the centre of attention You no longer place yourself in a position of authority, you recognize that we're as a whole structure, with the intention of helping one another and grow. Your well-being is closely tied to yours. Consider it this in this way: If you consider you are the centre of the universe then any difficulty you encounter could be one on a global scale, and therefore of severe significance and even death. If you are serving the greater good, your attention gets turned away from you and to the larger good. Attention is as a magnifying glass. If you examine yourself using an magnifying glass, then each issue you face appears to be the ultimate goal of your world.

Be Courageous and Accept Some Risks

Courage is an attribute, and often, life calls for the courage to act. Everyone has the capacity to show courage. We don't want that you become Joan of Arc but I would like you to take a stand and develop in yourself the virtue of courage. It is a virtue you can develop within your.

I love skiing for example. The sport can be risky however does this mean that I should avoid skis? No. Skiing is a great way to experience many pleasures, and if I'm prudent, the risk is minimal, so I have that I have the confidence to consider these dangers and instead enjoy the sport.

Risks are part of living that we must be a person who doesn't take risks. There are risks that you face every day but you don't admit that they are risks simply because you're a bit smug and think there are other issues priority to pay focus. Similar to that, it is important to recognize that by not constantly monitoring your life the risks are there; it is important to be prepared to accept these risks as majority of individuals on the earth...

Recognizing that you wear an electronic watch throughout the day will captivate your attention but are you allowing this to happen? Attention is an expensive and scarce resource. You don't get to enjoy an unlimited amount. Make wise use of it! The scope of our attention is only limited, and every second we have to decide the direction we want to take it. Anything we are unable to admit to, it doesn't mean it doesn't exist. This is just not a something we are aware of as we currently perceive it. While I write this article, do you think there is radiation in the air because or an incident at the nearby nuclear facility I'm unaware of? This could be true however, it's extremely unlikely. If it's true or not I can say for certain that it doesn't exist because I have chosen not to create the existence of it in my own perception of real. How do you feel this relates to your own? It is a shame that you are paying excessive attention and energy at the possibility of becoming sick, but failing to recognize the illness in time or even at all. If you experience a headache that is quite frequent, there is a choice to not the possibility of identifying it as a possibility; it's most likely caused by insufficient amount of sleep or an excess of focus. It is not often due to some infectious illness or disease But do you pay attention? It is possible of it happening, but there is a low risk and you need to possess the sense and confidence to realize that the chances are not significant enough to be concerned about the headache. Take Tylenol and go on and on with your day. If you're relaxed confident, focused, optimistic and confident, and the pain persists for a few days, then it might be worth taking a closer look, the same way as you would. If your pain has become paralyzing, it is a sure sign that there's no doubt of that. Go get examined.

I'm not saying that there's no rule book, the way to respond to a sign calls for a judgement and some degree of wisdom, but it is impossible to make a correct judgment when you're stressed and anxious. The courage of a person will take away the majority anxiety that you are prone to. You must faith that, if you experience some medical issue, there are obvious indicators that are triggering you to take action.

I'm just as committed and eager as you to be healthy but I have decided to not pay consideration to the majority of small ailment I see within my body. Do I put myself in danger? Maybe, However, this does not suggest that I'll wind with a disease and you'll be. However, I am able to affirm that I'm living more content as I'm focusing my energy towards things I love, rather than aspects that make me anxious.

Chapter 5: Hope and Human Potential

The advancements in the field of medicine is something that you must be aware of in your head because it's an actual fact, and a solid foundation of hope that isn't rooted in the realm of religion or mysticism.

Apart from that aside from that, I would like you to be aware that in the event of a sickness, there are many more ways to be hopeful. If there's existence, there's a chance. If you have enough determination with positive thoughts and a empowering set of belief, you'd probably have one of these remarkable story-telling success stories, amazing self-healing stories (that occur frequently throughout everyday life) should you suffer from an illness that killed you. The illness itself is just one aspect of the tale as "cure, human potential, miracles, medicine, and hope" is a different one, just as significant, as, if not greater.

In reality, most times it is not necessary to require a lot of effort in cultivating this positive attitude, like I said previously, both science and medicine possess extraordinary abilities.

If, for instance, you're concerned about not contracting the potentially fatal illness at the right time, you should remember the story of the child, Dale Ostrander, who drowned in the frigid Pacific He was saved after just fifteen minutes in the water and was able to recover.

Do not tell me there's any hope. The scenarios that you imagine might be not a source of hope. But it is true that there is always a chance to be hopeful. Even If you don't admit it, that doesn't necessarily mean that it's not true. The stories of miracles aren't as unlikely as the dire scenario you might think of yourself as.

I can't remind you enough of just how awesome the human capacity is. Humanity's potential is endless If you could combine all the talents of the amazing people in the world in one single person, that individual would be an actual god. If you were able to spare the time, you could have all of these talents - technically, making you a living god. Take a look at the amazing athletes across a variety of sports and arts and look at these extraordinary people and see what they achieve with their brains and their bodies. Human potential is endless which is why you're an exceptional human being. Don't tell me that the body you've been given is incapable to heal itself or perform incredible things. The majority of them have been born just exactly like us They were able to achieve this capacity through determination, willpower to think positively and the ability to train. The only thing you could have left out is training.

The rest is within your immediate access and instruction, I suggest you begin today if you haven't start it.

Don't Take Life Too Seriously; Laugh When You Can

My best suggestion I can offer is to not be too serious about your life, keep a positive attitude be happy as you can, and smile at things whenever you get an opportunity to. If you've got a pimple or mole which you're concerned about, take the time to be jolly for a few minutes, then be jolly about how you feel about the situation for a second; it is time to go back to thinking of it as a potentially deadly tumor.

Make fun of yourself and do it in a kind way. If you've got a tiny pimple that appears on the nose, smile at your own perception in the form it might have been: "Oh this is the Ziganga virus! I'm going to die tomorrow...ooooo" (I am sure it's tempting to search for the disease on the internet as I made it up from scratch!).

You must stop looking at the situation in such a horrifying but fatalistic angle and consider that until now, you've worried for five years, and nevertheless, you're still here and, most likely, in good well-being; that's kind of hilarious, isn't it?

Hypochondria is Weak

Parasitic Behaviour

If you are thinking about it, hypochondria may not an enemy that is powerful. It triggers negative thoughts, which have no basis in fact and is largely dependent on the enticement of your focus. Attention does not necessarily mean recognizing its existence, however the presence of the other components it requires you to consider. If you choose not to use or give away the ability to pay attention, it would not have basis to exist.

Hypochondria can't make decisions or draw scary conclusion on its own. it relies on the capabilities of your brain with which you hold the power. Don't fool yourself into thinking that you control your mind's attention. You may be astonished whenever thoughts arise, but you are able to choose whether to let it linger within your mind for hours or ignore it. That is to say, you have no control over the development of the stimulus, but only the persistence of it. A little more on that in the future...

The issues you're considering, in regards to your body, occur since you be aware of them. I can't imagine how many of pimples, irritations and signs you may have missed throughout your lifetime due to your focus to another thing like a pimple irritation, mole... Are they worthwhile to ignore? Most likely, as many circumstances you're paying your attention are worth ignoring and probably not worth your time even.

Conditional Existence

Have you noticed that your anxieties, feelings of your health and degree of your illness depend heavily on your mood and the condition you're in? There is a tendency to think throughout the day about a discomfort or pain, and worry about health-threatening illnesses and this can create an immense place in your range of concerns and consciousness. The pimple on your arm appears to you as if it's the beginning of a cancer that demands urgent attention. This causes you fighting for your survival and creates a sense of fear, despair and anxiety. In the evening, you're invited for meal at a friend's home You are exhausted and don't really wish to attend because you're in not an excellent state of mind (which is not unusual considering you've been fretting about your condition for the entire day!) But, in the fear of dissappointing your pal, you agree to make it. It's a few drinks, get to meet fascinating people, and despite the initial desire to not put in any effort or to keep praising yourself, and not smiling you are able to have fun. You joke, you laugh while your mind is diverted somewhere else and then you've totally forgotten about the pimple. The similar biological set-up and mental tendencies, but your hypochondriac thoughts are unable to even exist. How come? Your attention/awareness has been placed on something else and have not handed your attention to the hypochondria.

What is the reason why in this moment, you are not thinking that your existence is in danger? The reason why you decided not to grant Hypochondria control over your life? What caused your priorities to shift? It is true that you will never know whether our lives are by any means in any particular moment or time. There are too many unanswered questions and underlying factors that we are able to only pray that with the highest probability our belief that this isn't the case however, we can't endure this anxiety. choosing to enjoy and live life despite any risks We decide to not place this issue on the top of our list which is an appropriate attitude. The influence of certain variables in our life is influenced by what we give priority to these parameters. When you were eating at a restaurant, you had no intention of deciding that health was not something you should give importance to, and you had no choice but to attend. You became distracted, and as a result your hypochondria was at that moment no ability to affect your life due to the fact that the factor (your health) is able to exercise influence over you did not have any significance in the context of your priority.

Imagine you're an firefighter who suffers from hypochondria, and you have to rescue the people in a building that was burning. While you are on the job you will think about your health as the last thing that you'll think about. The shift in your priorities are due to the circumstance you're in. it is your responsibility to protect the people. It doesn't mean that the health of your family isn't important However, it is a sign you are in a moment where you have decided not to pay your health attention because other issues are more important.

It is unlikely that you will always have the possibility of being caught up in similar circumstances so you will need the power of your mind, your set of belief and principles to assume the responsibility in this stimuli that will motivate you to shift your focus away from worrying about your well-being. It is also possible to generate your own sources of distraction. What do you need to do? The key is be convinced that living a life essential and you must act in a way that is consistent with your beliefs. Take whatever action is necessary in order to be happy, as well as make your loved ones satisfied as well.

Chapter 6: An Unfounded Fear

It is not my intention to claim that hypochondria causes your unfounded fear since you do not have illness (I would be willing to join your for a second accepting the fact that we will never have the ability to confirm if it's actually the case) however, the reason is that the core of your anxiety isn't wanting to forfeit your life, and by acting as if you do, you're in fact not.

If you are thinking about death by thinking about death, you unleash the power of death into your life; You already draw those things you are afraid of similar to how contemplating a happy moment will bring you with a smile, or that is, the effect the moment made on you. The idea of dying influences your mental state and can trigger a series of negative feelings. The thought of death can cause you to be in the state of being in a state of mental trance and will rob you of the desire to live and will obstruct your desire to develop and grow. This is not to say that you shouldn't be afraid of death, but rather: "go and put your life at risk!" That would go against living in the present and honoring the fact that you exist as a physical entity.

Here's my question which one are you scared of losing? Are you scared of having to go through a lifetime of anxiety? Are you scared of living an existence of constant anxiety and depression? Are you scared of losing your joy? If so you should begin attracting happiness by attracting joy instead of dreading the loss of something you don't already have.

The situation you frequently are in is likely worse than dying; therefore, why are you afraid of dying? Have you experienced so painful and depleting states of mind which can become more debilitating... Therefore, get up because you've experienced everything!

A Condition Fuelled By Our Knowledge

Did you know about the saying "ignorance is bliss"? It is also true for hypochondria, where the more you don't are aware, the less to worry about. The reason we are afraid of a particular condition because we've heard all the time about it and are aware of how dangerous it is. However, in certain regions of the world, there are people who don't fear it because they've not heard of the disease. Certain diseases can be as terrifying, and even more dangerous than the ones that we are most likely to hear about, but we don't really fear due to the fact that we don't ever hear of.

We are concerned about the toxins we consume within our foods, we are concerned about carcinogens, and we worry about everything that is to be worthy of our attention, however there are a lot of aspects we do not hear about that we should be concerned about and which we don't be afraid of simply because we're not aware of them. We should not have to blame ourselves for not being concerned about them, and there is no reason not to. Many of us feel that we're at ease when in reality there is no control. For instance, one might be aware that certain food items contain carcinogenic components and try to avoid these, yet eat items that have a higher risk of causing cancer and feel reassured as the knowledge didn't reach the person. However, the truth is that the avoidance of certain foods could be advantageous however it could also be insignificant within the bigger perspective. Certain people lived extremely long lives, without abide by any specific form of advice that promotes cautiousness. There are numerous things that you can take to protect the health of his family without stressing over specifics.

Self- diagnostics

Most likely, you will use symptoms to feed and reinforce your anxiety and you may even resort to self-diagnoses even though you are not educated to make such decisions. What is the reason doctors are trained for years, in the event that they could comprehend the human body's anatomy with such effortlessness?

It is often difficult to recognize the body's reactions that cause symptoms and are usually related to a myriad of factors, ailments and in many occasions, aren't able as a diagnostic tool for a specific condition. Symptoms can be induced by psychosomatic/psychological factors as much as they can be induced by foreign organisms/compounds intruding the body.

Many symptoms aren't specific to one condition and the same symptoms may be shared by various diseases or conditions. If you've been spending for hours in front of a computer monitor all day long, you're likely to experience headaches. The headache can be a sign that should be alarming to you?

Make Hypochondria Your Best Friend

A Competitive Advantage

The first thing to remember is that it is important to not view your illness as negatively as you may. The conditions you have been suffering from has led you to acquire a variety of skills that are able to use to your benefit. Even though it's challenging you, but it also offers you many possibilities.

Realising the Manifestation Powers You Have

The condition you're suffering from has caused you to be aware of the amazing manifestation capabilities of the brain. Or just put, the astonishing ability that the brain has. It is possible that you have manifested the majority of your anxieties as physical manifestations in the absence of any illness. Aren't you amazed? Imagine what you could accomplish if you were able to transform your obsessive thoughts to a more positive outlook and apply all that focus on good work as well as productive actions. Have you tried your hand at the power of this brain; very few people are able to discover our incredible abilities that we're blessed with. It is now time to be energized more than ever before to use your brain to the best application and anticipate the very best results to come your way.

Better Know Yourself

You've been forced to contemplate on numerous occasions the best way to come from this situation, to know what your worries are and to consider the reason you're facing these inner challenges. Your inner reflection and questions will help you understand your self in a way that is remarkable. If you can reduce your thoughts of hypochondriacs knowing yourself can give you an important advantage in life. This procedure will have led to the development of a certain level of emotional control.

Attention to Details, Directing Focus

A little bit of humour I'm sure that continuously keeping an eye on your body and observing your health has helped you develop a keen eye to the details, and has helped you learn to be focused. It is always possible to make usage of this talent. Concentrate your attention elsewhere and let it work its work.

Motive to Investigation and Research

The stress you are feeling has likely resulted in you trying to learn more about your symptoms by reading, asking questions or searching for information and doing additional research regarding your health condition. There are times when you can devote hours to online studying about different diseases. You know what, this can be a helpful device that could use towards fuelling your interest rather than stoking your anxieties.

A Life Changer

Here is where all beauty is created. It is our mission on this planet to develop as well as fulfill a goal. Perhaps you're not sure the purpose of your life but you haven't contemplated it. But when you have freed your mind and energy that on worrying and pondering, I urge to think about it; because, to evolve in the world without having a goal is similar to sailing on the seas without a compass or a way to navigate.

It's true, the condition of hypochondria can be exhausting. It's every day, taking your thoughts and time Sometimes, it seems like you'd rather think about something else However, those thoughts worry about are always coming at your mind. It's no wonder that you are thinking of bigger plans... If you had the desire to, realization of this could be a sigh of relief and a pain by itself.

Agonies and hardships, come to us to teach us lessons. They serve an objective; they teach us humility and help open our hearts to compassion and helping those around us. The challenges and obstacles cause us to face these obstacles and overcome the issues. There is need for solutions, and these solutions form the heart of the growth of mankind and civilisation.

Hypochondria can trigger in you the need for ways to remain secure and safe as well as the need to overcome fears, and master your thoughts, and the desire to enjoy a happy, healthy and calm mind. These are all important evolution elements for humans which is why they call for personal growth could not have tried if you weren't in a position to. Begin to realize the value of your situation and begin taking note of it and smile and say: "I understand what you tried to convey to me and now it's the right time to get moving. ..."

An Enemy You Cannot Defeat

It is not worth creating hypochondria as a foe when you are in a an offensive position, oppose it, and then send it negative thoughts, you'll exhaust your body while feeding it with negative thoughts. You're like you were fighting, but denying your part.

It is important to recognize the fact that, at present, a part of who you are. It is a part of who you are and it is important to remain patient because it is likely to align with your real nature and alter itself. Your self-love should be so much that you are happy with the person you are, with all of your talents and strengths, despite your flaws. Do not get angry or upset whenever hypochondriac thoughts return to you. Acceptance and surrender are the key. Relax, be patient and respectful to yourself. affirm yourself with "Ah I'm looking forward to your silly hypochondria! I haven't had to bother you for some time!"

If you were a parent who was afraid of ghosts and turns to you for comfort and comfort, would you be annoyed but rather accept his vulnerability and fear, and work to aid the child? Think about hypochondria as one of the parts of you which is trying to inform that you are in the wrong.

When your hypochondriac thinking kicks into your head, say:

"I am very happy with myself. I have a few fears, but that's okay There is no reason to be worried... I am a healthy body's still functioning and I'm able to use the strength within me to take action that is worthy of my time, regardless of what the condition or pain that has me in it, I have the ability to fight any condition and no one could ever take away my desire for peace within and having a fulfilling life. If I am forced to stay alive for another two days, I'm going be sure to get the most of them."

The great thing about this person you may consider to be your adversaries is that by now, you'll be able to recognize it thoroughly. You are aware of the possibility that it could attack... But where can you find the excitement to this? One of the factors that win many combats is the element of shock that hypochondria doesn't control over your. It is a weapon you know and how it impacts your. Be prepared whenever you face a situation that is stressful, take a deep breath, and relax. Smile... Relax, close your eyes whenever you get an opportunity to reconnect with yourself, locate your strength and think about all the things we've talked about in the past: the human capacity, statistics optimism, faith and the most important of all, your brand new beliefs. If you create a major statement about your situation, it'll be a huge issue in your daily life. If you focus your energy on acknowledging your illness "I am a hypochondriac" and it takes on disproportionate shapes!

It is clear that making hypochondria your adversary is futile, should you not consider making hypochondria your best friend? Think of it as a friend that helps you understand your own and inspires you to grow as well as a person that teaches you to be in control of your own existence, to be brave and show compassion for those around you.

Chapter 7: Wake-up And Take Your Life in Your Hands!

Your mindset, awareness your beliefs, mindset and your state of mind are crucial that can turn any circumstance to turn it into an opportunity for learning. Understanding certain situations requires the use of tools and instruction. After I've covered the mindset and rationale that you must adopt in order to resolve your problem and the factors you must believe in within your mind, it's now time to get involved and be a logical person in recognizing the resources available to you and take advantage of them. Don't be a passive observer and hope that things will change and I urge you to look forward towards the day when you'll no longer have to suffer from the symptoms of hypochondria. In addition, I ask you to commit yourself, discipline, and determination. Each of the suggestions and suggestions will force that you take action. Your first step to take your life back is by reading the book. Recognize that at this point there is no time to be completely passive. The feeling of being awestruck, fearless, and invisibly is a condition which requires constant effort until momentum has been built as well as the joys of daily actions begin fueling the feeling. Therefore, get up and start taking action!

If you've found this book useful, make sure to go to my website:

www.marktheway.com

It is also possible to take a look at my Life Transformation course I've published on Udemy.

Being a certified coach I offer coaching one-on-1 services. Please don't hesitate to get in touch with me and discuss the ways in which I can help with this:

info@marktheway.com

Adopt the Proper Mindset, the Relevant Principles and an Empowering System of Beliefs

In the beginning, you must take all possibilities at your disposal in order to solve your issue. It is essential to confront your situation with determination with positive attitude and determination. Do, every single day, what is necessary to be reminded of the concepts I've mentioned previously. It's a matter of determination and commitment to take your life back into your own hands.

I would strongly recommend you listen to motivational speakers like Tony Robbins. There's plenty of information online for free, and information that can teach you how to handle your situation and boost your drive. I would highly recommend to do this. This is a mindset it is a total mindset must be embraced prior to focusing on hypochondria specifically. It is true that you've got your hypochondria problem to tackle before focusing on bigger concerns and taking care of issues in the world. That is incorrect - now is now more important than ever to concentrate on the bigger picture.

It is essential to convince yourself that you are not going to permit yourself to get sucked down or lost in something that does harm your best interests Your time is important and your focus is valuable and you must utilize them to the fullest extent possible. The process of building momentum isn't just a matter of simply reading this article and viewing a motivational video and you will not get the benefits of engaging in this. It will take time andinvesting in the concepts and inspiration to be absorbed into the mind of your. It is essential to be into the right mindset that this mental state must occur in your daily routine!

Your first agenda is to view an inspirational video each day It won't fix your issue but can make significant impact on finding a solution. It is my request that you prepare a daily calendar which you'll put a note on each day when you've watched an appropriate video or access to relevant content. Be an active participant by noting your favorite ideas and resonate with. I would like you to be feeling amazing and understand all the motivations for feeling that way!

Chapter 8: What exactly is hypochondria?

Hypochondria is among the most fascinating illnesses known to mankind and is well into the days of traditional medicine.

The phrase "Hypochondria" is Greek and refers to something similar to "under the cartilage". The cartilage that surrounds the ribs is referred to as this since it was believed that the region surrounding the diaphragm could be described not just as the center of the spirit, but as the place where melancholy was a common occurrence.

It was a belief that remained in force throughout the 19th Century. Then, different interpretations that suggested that hypochondria could be "the mildest form of madness" it was a form of "melancholy", or a "partial occurrence of neurasthenic syndrome".

We now know that hypochondria is an anxiety about disease or being sick. If you experience this condition, you may believe that you're suffering from the most severe type of illness through being aware of the smallest change of your body's bodily activities.

In a constant manner, or at times in a series of the thoughts of your mind are constantly occupied and you are convinced that you're suffering from a severe illness. Common colds could be an indication of an illness that causes a severe immune response like AIDS and headaches can be a sign of brain tumours. constipation is a sign that colon cancer is present. These are just some of the many examples.

The patient either visits doctors frequently for a check-up of his symptoms or avoids visiting the doctor, simply because they fear having the results of his worries verified.

The fear that is a result of illness that can drastically reduce the quality of living, may be similar to panic attacks. Hypochondria, however, is thought as a psychosomatic disorder. It is a psychosomatic illness which can cause physical manifestations. A patient, for instance might be sceptical that he suffers from a tumor on the bladder. While focusing on his bladder's activity, the behavior of the bladder can change due to the fact that the person is experiencing stress, but not due to a physical illness. However, the patient believes that their suspicions are verified.

There's a lot of debate about whether hypochondria can be classified as psychosomatic, as the physical symptoms aren't an essential cause for it, however they often occur in conjunction with the illness.

Secondary hypochondria

If there's a major disease, such as schizophrenia or an anxiety disorder or schizophrenia, and the resulting hypochondria stems from the illness, it is called in medical terms a hypochondria secondarily. The symptoms are not a sign of illness.

What is the best time to be hypochondriac?

The word 'hypochondria' can be quite wide. It starts with the awareness of self-health and the practice precautionary measures, however it may lead to hypochondriacal manic episodes.

The people who listen to their body's signals, are taking the health of their bodies seriously. But, the threshold to becoming a hypochondriac doesn't seem distant. The hypochondriac person isn't a one who is taking vitamins every day, or worries that he might have an itch following a swim prior to. If you're a hypochondriac are more likely to be worried like, say, the fact the possibility of having an illness that is serious or cancerous.

The first thing you think of when your first waking up is "How do I feel?". If you think to your self "Are the headaches or stomach pains strong today?" Or "Is my hand shaking more today? " This implies that your thoughts are hypochondriacal. Your life and thoughts have a constant fear. It is probably the largest contrast between hypochondriacs and an individual who is health conscious. They can lead a life that is well-balanced way, without ever suffering from thoughts of negativity.

What exactly defines the line of demarcation and when will it begin to become a disease? This is usually a difficult thing to determine.

Are you a hypochondriac?

Are you ever unsure what your behavior might be normal or if you're already hypochondriac? Are others around you believe you're hypochondriac?

The line between health and disease is often not evident. Everybody worries from time moment about their well-being. The first sign that you're not living up to the rules is if you find you are causing your mind to make you sick, or you're unable to perform tasks that you used to be able to do. Also, perhaps the way you interact with others has altered.

Self-test

The self-test below can provide you with an indication of whether the way you react to illnesses are normal or more likely a hypochondriacal disease.

The test will only provide you an idea about your present condition but it isn't a replacement for the diagnosis of an expert psychologist or physician. It is not necessary that each of the symptoms listed has to be attributed to hypochondria. Always consult with an expert about the cause. If you are concerned that you suffer from hypochondria, I recommend insistently that you locate someone who is an expert in this field.

This test is not appropriate for people who are chronically sick or sick, those with a medical diagnosis for proof or those who have recovered or are recovering from serious illnesses.

You must answer the questions below by answering the following questions with "yes" or "no". Keep track of the amount of instances you've answered "yes". You should answer the question in a hurry, not worrying too much about the questions.

Are you constantly worried whether you might have an unavoidable illness?

Are you suffering from a variety of kinds of pains, or symptoms of illness?

Are you constantly noticing changes in the bodily functions you perform? (digestion, heart)

If you learn from your friends or in the press regarding a health issue is it possible about the possibility that you suffer from the same illness?

Are you concerned the people around you don't take the time to consider you even when you're sick?

Are you skeptical of your doctor's words when he assures you that everything is in order?

Do you believe that you are more concerned regarding your health than most individuals?

Do you worry you have something serious in your body that isn't right, yet, despite this, medical professionals do not seem to be able to recognize it?

Are you able to control your pulse or blood pressure or conduct self-tests?

Are you prone to changing your physician simply because you don't feel confident in the doctor?

Analysis:

You've completed all of the questions. Find out how many times have replied using "yes". The amount of "yes" answers will give you an indication of the current state.

1. Everything is good! Most likely, you don't have hypochondria. The way you

feel about your body are in the normal range. There are times when you worry from time the other regarding your well-being. There are times when you think there is a problem and then it goes away. You may have altered your physician since you didn't trust the doctor, but this isn't a frequent occurrence. A sense of responsibility towards the health of your body is crucial. Maintain it!

3 to 4: Caution! Your body listens to it intensely and seem to be extremely sensitive the processes it goes through. The condition can be a hindrance at times throughout your day activities however, it doesn't dictate what that you perform. I suggest speaking with an expert psychologist or a physician so that you can avoid any increase in symptoms.

5 to 10: Warning! Fear of getting sick can affect your thinking and behavior very intensely. Your well-being and life could be

severely impacted because of your fears about illness. If you've never spoken to a medical professional who is qualified about your symptoms or feelings I suggest that you speak with a physician or psychologist as soon as you can.

What is the prevalence of hypochondria?

Through time, there have been cases of hypochondriacs. Examples include Charlie Chaplin, Frederick the Great, Woody Allen and Thomas Mann.

Here are some statistics to show the prevalence of hypochondria may be higher than you might think.

In Germany about one percent of people is suffering from hypochondria. It's about 820,000!

The most severe type that is the hypochondriacal disorder is experienced by around 0.5 percent. It is about five out of 10,000 persons affected. (In Germany, that amounts around 4,100).

A little over 6% Germans are affected by some kind of mild health-related concerns.

The majority of people who are universities for psychotherapeutic therapy are hypochondriacs.

Amid 2% to 7% of the patients who visit German doctors are hypochondriacs.

Similar numbers of both men as well as women are affected by hypochondria.

The exact number of patients can be difficult to calculate since there's very not much research conducted in this area and also because many sufferers don't get help from a professional in fear of embarrassing themselves.

There is a possibility of a huge quantity of unrecorded instances. A lot of sufferers don't go to the doctor for anxiety of getting confirmation of their illness and therefore, they're not recorded by the system of health and not included in the statistical records. In most instances those who suffer from the illness tend to see a doctor more frequently. It also places a huge burden on the financial system.

Who are the people most affected?

As of now there are no precise figures publicly available regarding the age at which sufferers are diagnosed at the time that illness first manifests. A third of the people who were questioned said that they already had fears of specific illnesses during their growing up.

However, it can be claimed that both females and males are affected by the disease.

There are some people who have hypochondriacal attacks following an illness that is serious. The most common are those recovering from an illness that was serious and are concerned about getting a second relapse or developing a new illness. It could turn into hypochondria since they are aware of their body's processes thoroughly and are very extremely sensitive to changes.

Individuals who witness the grave disease of someone close to them can develop hypochondriacs. They are concerned about their health. increase and, in a flash new symptoms become apparent, that might be similar to those of the person who is sick or be signs of a different disease.

Individuals who have lost confidence in health systems or their doctors due to inaccurate diagnoses or the late detection of an illness, could be in a state of.

A few sufferers might have had a traumatizing experience. The trauma can be a factor in the formation of hypochondria.

Also, it is possible to experience the hypochondria phases due to increasing access to the latest information regarding illness and health. The majority of these are medical students and those that are undergoing training in healthcare sector, for example nursing personnel. It's not unusual to find students who are studying about a specific illness suffering from the same symptoms they're studying about. The majority of times, this will be a temporary occurrence and it will disappear quickly.

Research shows that the majority of viewers of the health programs on television get sick following the program's conclusion and fret more about the possibility of suffering from an illness.

It is a condition that could affect anybody regardless of whether they've had any medical education, had a prior disease or any other like that.

What subtypes exist?

There are several sub-groups in hypochondria. They differ through their signs. Their treatment, however, is identical to the "classical" hypochondriac.

On the next pages in the following pages, the principal hypochondria sub-groups are described short.

The olfactory-reference disorder

The olfactory reference disorder is also referred to as Bromosis, is the constant mistaken belief that a person emits an abnormal scents that people with this condition believe is offensive and unpleasant to others.

The cause of this disorder could be linked to other chronic diseases like disordered thinking, compulsive or schizophrenia, or an injury that is organic on the brain.

A patient may have an impression that movements, facial expressions and behavior of others originate from their offensive smell of his body.

Most often, the odor is followed by the constant search for organic ailment, which could provide the explanation for this subjectively observed smell of the body.

A lot of people are addicted to scents and deodorants in order to disguise their scent. Fear of offending other people can negatively affect the social life for the person suffering, they feel embarrassed and withdraw from social interactions. They don't feel comfortable to interact with other people.

Delusional parasitosis

Simply put, it is the skin-insect-syndrome, also known amongst experts as Parasitosis. The condition occurs when a person is misinformed about the fact that living organisms such as insect-like worms, spiders and worms can be seen on the skin and in motion. This can cause fear as well as itching.

The most probable causes for this disorder are the abuse of cocaine and amphetamine addiction, as well as the withdrawal of alcohol with delirium as well as disorders of the central nervous systems as well as brain injury.

Dysmorphophobia

The people who are affected by the condition, are convinced that they're either cursed and/or disfigured or malformed or are just plain unattractive. They're obsessed with thinking that even every slight deviation from normal, like losing hair or having a mole could result in serious negative consequences. It can have a detrimental impact on their work and social daily.

Bowel movement hypochondria

For this kind of hypochondria, special attention is given by the patient to movements to the toilet. The patient is focused on only his digestion, and knows precisely the time and frequency it has gone going to the bathroom. The patient will pay close careful attention to the nature of the bowel movements as well as any associated symptoms for example, gas release.

Afraid of getting sick

Fear of sickness is described by medical professionals as nosophobia. It is a type of hypochondriacal disorder which lasts for a long time but does not always create an extreme anxious condition. In spite of the name, it's not a disorder of phobia as such in the strict sense of the term however, it's an anxiety disorder.

The people who suffer from nosophobia experience high-risk of believing, or having faith that they are suffering from a condition regardless of the fact that there is none, or very few tangible medical indicators.

The person suffering from the condition is extremely aware of every bodily function and is extremely sensitive to things that aren't in line with normal. However, it is possible that this can be interpreted incorrectly or inaccurately which can lead to the person believing that he suffers from an illness, even though there are no evidence of it.

The sufferer, however, has no reason to believe that he is deluded. He is aware that there are no evidence of the fears he has. This is the main difference between someone who suffers from nosophobia and those suffering hypochondria. Hypochondriacs can't distinguish between fear of sickness or the sickness. Hypochondriacs are convinced that they are suffering from the illness and feel symptoms. But, despite the fact that they realize they're suffering due to the fear of illness and not the actual illness, it's still an agonizing experience. The anxiety is unfounded, but it is impossible to break away from thoughts that are swirling all around you regarding the illness.

The condition isn't in any way to confuse with mysophobia regardless of whether both conditions typically occur together. If you suffer from mysophobia you're scared of getting infected by bacteria or germs due to dirty food, bad dirt or trash, and or even believing that you suffer from an health condition. It is possible to experience short anxious attacks in the wake certain events.

Hypochondriamic environmental

If you are suffering from environmental hypochondria then the principal cause of your anxieties is your environment. In the past, these concerns could be based on lightning or thunder, which appeared to be threatening. People today are concerned more about being negatively affected by electromagnetic waves like electro smog, radioactive radiation, or the chronic poisoning brought on by for instance amalgam. Different chemical compounds such as those that can be deemed as allergenic, may also trigger anxieties and fears.

The one thing that all influences from the environment can cause are all based on is that they're unobservable and can't be proved. As opposed to obvious causes that have negative effects on the human body, for instance smoking, alcohol, sun or gas, invisibly non-controllable causes are believed as a bigger risk.

There are groups of interest, that make the hypochondria of the environment more severe, such as due to their active appearance in the media trying to gain acceptance of their views.

Cyberchondria

The expression "cyberchondria" is derived from the terms "cyber" and "hypochondria" and refers to a physical condition of stress in individuals which is caused by an overly-focused search for symptoms on the web. Hypochondriacal traits that are already evident of the patient are heightened due to the development of cyberchondria. It is the modern version of hypochondria.

It's likely that you've seen that: you quickly take off your cell phone and make a note of your symptoms, and in minutes you are presented with many possible illnesses according to the symptoms you've entered. A thorough search for the information contained found in medical texts is gone from the past. The majority of the information today can be found on the internet since it's fast and easy.

The internet is a great resource for research. It isn't always easy, however there is a confusing range of health information. Additionally there are many sources that may not be credible.

Hypochondriacs are often afflicted with you are frightened of information that is available from sufferers and comments posted on chats and forums makes the issue worse. When you are reading about someone else with a similar illness it gives you the impression of being more real as opposed to reading only texts about the illness. You are able to identify with the person and his illness, and your belief in that the illness is real grows dramatically.

If you're one of us with no expertise Internet research can prove helpful in classifying your ailments and getting ideas on how to treat. But for those who have an fears of illness the internet can be risky due to the variety of information available is disorienting and fears that you have may appear to be verified.

The illness could get worse or aggravated by using the internet. In addition it is possible to run into the possibility of addiction. This is a result of spending hours on the internet every all day.

Chapter 9: How can hypochondria be manifested?

One of the most important characteristics of hypochondriacs is their anxiety about sickness. Apart from their fear of illness, they are also afraid of suffering, disability suffering, and even death.

There are symptoms that you're experiencing and the anxiety you experience as a result of it can be quite impossible to bear. There is a strong desire to discover what's the cause of your discomfort. The symptoms you experience on the physical side appear to be getting worse and you're looking at the slightest alteration in the body.

If you are a hypochondriac, then you experience symptoms that you associate with a particular disease and believe that you suffer from it. Insecurity and stress that this can cause could lead to anxiety attacks.

It can drastically impact your lifestyle If you're constantly worried about a disease inside your body. It is common to spend lots of time searching for information and gathering data on the symptoms you experience. You are consumed by fear of contracting this illness, and that consumes the majority of your hours of your day. It, in turn, affects your daily life in a significant way.

Be aware of the symptoms

You soon find yourself stuck in a vicious cycle that you'll have difficultly breaking out of. The first sign is that you are noticing each tiny change to your bodily processes, such as like skin rashes, swellings and rashes accumulation, a pounding heart or any minor discomfort. It is easy to find that the symptoms appear to be uncomfortable and you believe that it is an indication of illness.

Following that, you will begin to pay attention specifically at the area affected by your body. This in turn makes it more likely that you'll discover additional signs.

You also misinterpret signs because you believe they're result of a serious disease.

Examinations and observation get more frequent and additional measures are introduced, like weight-control or an intensive physical examination of affected zone.

The result causes the symptoms to become worse and making it worse by continuously looking at the affected part.

When you study symptoms that you notice, and to confirm that it could be caused by a serious condition is further strengthened, which raises the stress level.

Doctors visits

Patients with hypochondriac disease visit the doctor regularly. They seek to know which symptoms they're experiencing result of. In the process, they visit the physician more often. When the doctor states that the patient should not be concerned about the symptoms and is in good health This reassures the patient for a short time, but symptoms and anxieties return rapidly.

Patients do not feel that his physician is taking his concerns seriously, and this results in frustration and unhappiness. The patient often asks the following questions "Why does my doctor not recognise that I am suffering?". It then prompts him to look for a new doctor until the issue is "Which doctor, if any, will acknowledge that I am suffering? ", the same question is repeated constantly, whilst "doctor-hopping'.

Self-testing is a common practice for patients for signs of illness, like measuring pulse, blood pressure or self-palpation (poking in the spot affected). Family and friends are frequently requested to give their opinions on the possible signs of sickness. The same can cause anger, especially if the person suffering doesn't feel that the concerns of his family members are taken seriously.

They also have hypochondriacs who are averse to seeing a doctor or clinics, hospitals and even the cemeteries to avoid a confrontation with their fears, and to avoid getting their fears verified by a physician.

When a doctor prescribes treatment for a specific illness the likelihood is that the state of the patient gets worse and not improves. In some cases, negative side effects are brought about by taking medicines and make the illness worsen. A patient may notice the symptoms are not as obvious. The end result is not satisfactory, for both the physician and patient.

Health screening

A positive side of being hypochondriacs is that they lead very healthy lives. They rarely smoke or drink alcohol, as they fear the possibility of liver cancer or lung sclerosis.

The person suffering from the condition usually ensures to ensure he eats an appropriate diet, and that he may take part in sporting activities. In time the sufferer tends to engage in little or no exercise as he fears a decline in his physical health.

The patient hopes that by embracing the right lifestyle and habits will reduce the chance of developing a disease, and it is a factor he has the power to alter for him.

Insomnia and organs that are affected

The most commonly feared illnesses usually are serious illnesses. The most frequent cause is cancer that's the one most fearsome, and is being followed by heart issues and other disorders. Then there are diseases of the muscle or nervous system.

With the many cancer diseases the skin, brain lung and breast abdominal cancers are feared the most. Women are particularly at risk of developing cancers. often feared for gynaecological organs like the womb or ovary. Heart attacks as well as serious heart valve problems or aneurysms are the most probable heart problems that are suspected, whereas and ALS is the more probable neurologic conditions that are suspected by hypochondriacs.

In particular, when the fear of cancer-related illnesses like breast and skin cancer, the patient usually examines his body trying to find any signs of change. However, sometimes it can cause signs worse. In the case of example, if one studies his lymphatic glands by applying pressure to the lymphatic tissues and does the exercise frequently, since he believes they're constricted, this can result in lymphatic nodes becoming larger due to the continual tension exerted by the person suffering. The result causes anxiety to increase due to the fact that the lymph nodes become larger and will require more examinations.

Hypochondriacs are extremely well-informed regarding their supposed illnesses and, like for the case with lymphatic glands, the person suffering does not fabricate the symptoms; he's actually being affected by the symptoms.

For instance, the headaches are genuine, the heart beats can be detected easily and the trembling in the hands is easily observed by any person.

Chapter 10: What causes cause hypochondria?

There are a variety of theories related to the process by which hypochondria is developed. But the precise cause isn't yet clear. Furthermore, it's generally unclear whether hypochondria can be a disease on itself, or is the symptom of a different illness. If someone suffers from depression can suffer from hypochondria as an additional indicator. However there is a possibility that depression can develop as an outcome of hypochondria. If that is the scenario, it's hard to tell if depression or hypochondria are the cause of the illness.

The assumption is that hypochondria can develop as due to the interaction with a number of elements.

Triggers in childhood

There is a good chance that certain experiences from childhood may trigger hypochondria or it could be believed that there's a some deep psychological cause for it.

I will not discuss the subject in detail in this publication. If you're interested it, you will find an extensive quantity of writing regarding this subject. Instead, I'll give an overview of some of the most commonly used triggers in the pages below.

The experience of death and illness

Sometimes, there is an ancestor to past memories from childhood that can be linked to the fearful disease. If you have an intense fear of cancer, as an example there is a chance the person who was near to the person suffering had suffered, or actually was killed by it. The experience of facing death could transform and alter behaviour and thinking patterns which could lead to hypochondria later on.

Internal conflicts that are not resolved

If you have unresolved internal tensions, these may cause the mind to influence the body. The body, then reacts. Psychological issues are transmuted into physical issues and this is the reason why hypochondria can be described as a somatoform condition, due to the fact that there is no biological reason for physical signs.

The psychological issues manifest in physical signs. That is why hypochondria has been believed to be a self-medicating and self-healing method to deal with other issues. It is believed that this transition from the brain to body occurs during the early years of in the childhood.

Childhood was based upon fear

The environment a child grows up in as well as the conduct of parents may influence the growth of hypochondria later on in adulthood. Parents who were too cautious of their children, constantly worried that their child may be ill or injure itself, may result in limiting their child's freedom. If the child suffers from stress later in life, this may lead to the creation of a mental illness.

People who were taught from an early age to take care, and pay close focus on their health are more likely to experience more physical and mental symptoms as compared to others and have learned to attribute the signals a significant importance.

Influencing factors

The following elements can be helpful in causing hypochondria. There is no need for every factor to show up. They are just the common factors that are found in a study of the affected

Excessive belief in an existing sickness

The most significant reasons for the development of hypochondria could being a false belief about the presence of illness. The result is an overestimation of the severity and likelihood of a disease. A distorted interpretation of physical symptoms may determine the progression of hypochondria.

A low self-esteem

In general, people with hypochondria have low self-esteem compared to other individuals and are more fragile. Research has shown that there's a link with lower self-esteem as well as hypochondria. So, people who are prone to having low self-esteem, must be aware of hypochondriacal signs and strive to improve their self-esteem.

The desire for attention

Hypochondriacs have a greater demand for help and attention. It is possible that they've previously received much more attention while someone who is sick as opposed to what they normally would receive.

The amount of attention people initially receive for the illness, tends to diminish more and more as the time passes. When they realize, for the first time they are not confirmed by their doctor, other people in their vicinity are less attentive to their symptoms. Patients often hear phrases such as "I am sure it is nothing, last time the doctor said, you are healthy, do not worry".

There is a possibility that the patient then goes to the internet in lieu of his friends and family members for the attention they desire. The patient is able to participate for discussion on forums online, which allow a variety of people to speak and share opinions and ideas on their ailments.

Instability in the emotional department

When I say 'emotional stability' I am referring to the time when an individual stays stable and in a good place. In the initial stages of hypochondria it is not always an issue, meaning that the person is experiencing an imbalance within his mind which is known as neuroticism, in the technical sense.

The term "neuroticism" is frequently used in conjunction with

Insecurity

Anxiety

Inhibitions

Changes in mood

Nervousness

Vulnerability

If the emotional disorder becomes intense, the patient is extremely sensitive and has a very emotional reaction. Even things that others aren't likely to be concerned over, may lead a hypochondriac's mind to go out of control. Like, for instance: while other people could read quietly a book the hypochondriac could become angry over an newspaper article. It is more difficult for him to manage the stress levels of his body as compared to the majority of people. He is also quite prone to be nervous or frightened.

Blindness in the eyes of emotion

The difficulty in processing emotions is technically referred to as Alexithymia. In normal speech we speak of emotion the coldness of one's heart.

The past was when Alexithymia was thought to be an illness of personality that was also associated with psychosomatic signs. Nowadays, that notion is in doubt. This could be due to a lack or lack of emotion intelligence. In terms of emotional intelligence, I'm referring to an individual is capable of recognizing and defining one's own as well as other's emotions, but this isn't this case.

If a person suffers with Alexithymia It isn't capable of recognizing the emotions that he or others experience and is not competent in expressing these emotions. That is the reason we talk about a lack of emotional mental.

Around 10 percent of Germans have a condition known as the condition of emotional blindness. With one in 10 people suffer from it and it's possible you are familiar with someone who is affected or perhaps have it in your own life. Alexithymia is a condition that causes you to not recognize or communicate your personal emotions. It also means that you are unable to express emotions in words.

There are a few things that can be difficult:

Accepting your own feelings.

Influencing and shaping your personal emotions.

Being able to respond appropriately to an emotional incident.

Utilizing emotions to accomplish a task.

Ability to put yourself in the shoes that others are in so far as their opinions are in question.

Being aware of the emotions displayed by other people.

This can cause a variety of problems in daily life. It is the most important thing that impacts your social skills as your inability to understand other people's feelings can affect your social interactions.

It is crucial to remember that being blind to emotions is not a sign that you don't have feelings. It is just you are unable to recognize your feelings and are unable to express them in words.

Stress

Fundamental changes, stress or extreme events are usually the triggers for hypochondria phase. Stress may trigger physical signs that include irregular heartbeats or dizziness. Other symptoms include digestive problems or headaches. It's normal and could be due to the situation during the time.

If a person believes that there is a particular meaning behind the physical signs, in moments of stress or due to stress in itself the stress itself, it could lead to an incorrect interpretation of the reasons and a person may conclude the person is being affected by a specific illness.

The cycle continues In the end, stress triggers worry of being sick. Anxiety leads to an increase in anxiety level. This results in increased attention to the apparent illness. Patients then try to discover more details via the web or in textbooks and this confirms his suspicions, namely of having that specific disease. The signs continue to get worse as well as the stress that comes with having a serious illness and increases the level of stress again.

In my situation, the tension at work led me to experience headaches. The symptoms I experienced were thought to being a tumour in the brain. On the web, I discovered evidence to support my theory. This caused me to feel even more stressed which, in turn, caused even more headaches. It made me feel justified as I believed that I was suffering from illness.

That's how I discovered myself caught in the cycle of viciousness of life, which I was totally caught within. I didn't realize the fact that it was the stress which had led to the headaches. Probably tension headaches. This is a frequent occurrence.

Personal defence mechanisms that are not functioning properly

We all know that speeding at speeds of 180 km/h on the motorway can increase the chance of being involved in an accident. It is also known smoking cigarettes can lead to lung cancer. This is known, but lots of people continue to do it. Why? because we think that this won't occur to us. It's a type of defense mechanism for ourselves. This system isn't working well in those who suffer from hypochondriac disorders. When they are hypochondriacs those dangers that we recognize can become serious dangers. The changes we make in our perceptions can be the source of hypochondriacal signs and various psychological illnesses, according to a number of studies have proven.

Media

The media poses a significant risk for anxiety resulting from hypochondriacs either in the beginning, or by the case of a strengthening of existing hypochondriacal traits. The health and doctor shows constitute a significant part of what is on the television. Internet is also a great source of information. variety of information that can be difficult to take in.

Health management is an extremely discussed topic within the press. How do we recognize an illness in its beginning stage? Magazines, TV and the internet offer a variety of suggestions. In the present, it's the internet that is the most popular way to search for facts. This could cause or increase anxiety about a disease through a myriad of ways. The risk is the development of hypochondriacal behavior.

Additionally, students learn to take tests on themselves. It's all fine and healthy for healthy individuals to perform a specific quantity of self-testing to serve in order to protect themselves from sickness however, for hypochondriacs test, they can cause more harm than positive.

Experiences of personal illness

Experiences of illness in the early stages could be a factor in the formation of hypochondria. If someone has experienced one of these experiences prior to this for instance, having known that someone had illness that was discovered in the late stages or with symptoms that were not treated serious enough, then the fear of developing an illness can increase as a sense of distrust is built up towards doctors. If this causes an unfounded distrust in the medical field it can result in the appearance of hypochondriacal symptoms, as doctors cannot explain the signs, and patients are unable to trust the medical explanations provided by doctors.

Genetic Factors

It is not your birthright to be as a hypochondriac. But, genetics can play a role on anxiety-related symptoms. If one was born with an anxiety-related genetic condition the person is likely to be more susceptible to anxiety-related illnesses. But, genetically determined factors are not a major part in the formation of hypochondria. It is likely to result from external influence or the personal experience of the individuals.

Chapter 11: What is hypochondria? How can you tell?

It may take a lengthy period of time before the hypochondria one's own is identified. It can be particularly challenging if you as the person affected don't realize that you're not in a state of physical illness.

First aid usually will come from a general physician (GP). This is usually the one who you first go to. They are usually aware of the medical history of your family and is capable of describing the findings of any medical tests you have undergone. The doctor is the most qualified to determine if actual health concerns are present or if you're anxious about them.

If a doctor suspects hypochondria, he'll begin talking to you about it. He may then follow up with a treatment by psychologist or psychiatrist. To do this, you'll be required to sign a consent form and that means you must be able to see that something is that is not working.

Before beginning psychotherapy it is essential to establish confidence that you're free of any medical issue. It will involve a number of examinations and tests.

The psychiatrist will conduct an examination with the psychologist

When you first meet with a psychologist or psychiatrist during the first appointment, they will provide an extensive analysis basing his analysis on specific points in which you've spoken to the psychologist or psychiatrist.

Modern tests are utilized to establish a diagnosis. The tests are generally questionnaires in which a psychiatrist or psychologist can use to determine if hypochondria in the present, and if so the degree to which it's evident.

The test questions will be like those we have on our self-test. However, to determine the diagnostics, they'll be more specific.

The criteria for diagnosing

Hypochondria is recognized as a condition by World Health Organisation as an independently-caused illness. It is a condition that can be described as hypochondria when a person suffering from the condition frequently and overly worried about getting sick or becoming sick.

It is crucial to differentiate between the fear of being sick or getting sick as well as an extreme anxiety. For the diagnosis of hypochondria you must meet the following requirements of the American Diagnosis Catalogue (DSM-V) are required to be fulfilled:

An excessive worry of becoming sick or becoming unwell.

Physical symptoms do not exist and are usually only evident with a slight form. If the symptoms are severe there is a matter of personal preference on whether the concern is too much or not.

The person suffering from the illness has an elevated anxiety about sickness and can be easily stressed by medical issues.

A disproportionately negative attitude towards his health or avoidance of discussing the subject of health.

The fear must exist at a minimum of 6 months. The illness you are frightened of is not required to be the exact one.

Diagnostic tests have revealed no findings. There's no more plausible explanation of the symptoms other than hypochondria.

And, most importantly the fact that no anxiety or panic disorder is present.

Two divisions

There are generally two forms of hypochondria. The hypochondriac group wants their ailments to be looked at frequently and often requires medical help for example, going to the physician or specialist and also allows for technical information to be obtained for analysis, like X-rays or Computer Tomography scans. A different group is hesitant to go to the doctor at all costs due to the risk of being too high, and the suspect diagnosis will be verified.

The American classification system of psychological disorders categorizes hypochondria in different manner. There's a group called hypochondriacs who experience physical signs and symptoms, as well as those with a higher risk of suffering from anxiety.

The two types of divisions are similar. There is an individual who is worried about physical signs and would like to discuss them with a medical professional. Another group is the "silent" group, which is equally concerned about symptoms however, it is more afraid of knowing that there is a problem which is why they avoid seeking medical attention.

Other illnesses can cause a similar condition.

When making the diagnosis it is often difficult to determine if it's actually hypochondria or another condition. There are certain criteria which a physician can apply to differentiate between hypochondria from other illnesses.

These illnesses, which frequently are misunderstood as hypochondria, but require different treatment are discussed briefly and analyzed in the subsequent chapter. There is no way to go into more depth about the other illnesses in this article, as this book is focused on hypochondria. But, there's lots of fascinating literature on these other illnesses and goes into greater details about each diagnosis.

Hypochondriacal concerns with mild severity

In accordance with the criteria for diagnosis Hypochondria is a condition that has existed for a minimum of six months. It isn't the situation with minor hypochondriacal concerns. They can be experienced in a short duration and result in less effect on the everyday existence of those suffering. When we refer to symptoms that are only temporary signs, we do not talk about hypochondria, but rather the mild symptoms and are much simpler to manage.

Somatoform diseases

In contrast to hypochondriacs who is suffering from a somatoform disease exhibits distinctive physical signs. Hypochondria manifests more as belief or fear it is a belief that a person suffers from a severe illness instead of a particular sign or symptom. While these signs aren't caused by any kind of organic illness but they do occur more intensely by people suffering from it as opposed to those who suffer from hypochondria.

Disorders of the mind

True delusional disorder is unlike hypochondria, in that regardless of the number of tests that you take, you are unable to remain convinced of your beliefs. It is a certainty that you are sick, and are not going to change your mind. If you're a hypochondriac you could be able to, at a minimum for a brief period convince yourself that there is no evidence of negative findings from your medical tests. If you're delusional, that isn't possible anymore. The delusional disorder can be a result from hypochondria.

Disorder of panic

A panic disorder is usually focused on an event that is physical that is a cardiac an attack, or a heart problem. The focus is more on anxiety about a disease. You are now afraid that you will experience greater anxiety attacks. The panic attack becomes severe, however it does not last for time. They can, however, come back repeatedly and occur frequently. The name implies that this condition can be associated with intense anxiety in fear of losing your life.

General fear disorder

General fear disorder can be described as the fear of becoming seriously sick. This isn't what causes the anxiety. It is just one of the worries that the patient has. One could call it an umbrella term used to describe fears, of which hypochondria only makes up a tiny portion.

Phobia about illness

The fear of illness is akin to fear of contracting an illness. It is different in that in the case of illness phobia, it is the general worry about getting sick regardless of whether or not you're certain that you are suffering from an illness. The focus is not as much on symptoms, but greater emphasis on the need to be healthy. This could turn into a psychiatric habit. For instance, it may be the need to clean your hands regularly in order to keep your hands free of germs and viruses.

Compulsive disorder

Similar symptoms can be seen as that of a compulsive disorder. Like the anxiety of being sick sufferer of the disorder, the person suffering from compulsive disorders is driven, just as do hypochondriacs, to conduct himself in such a way so that he doesn't get sick at all in the first place. The person develops rituals of compulsive behavior to stay away from sickness, and this is why this condition distinguishes itself from hypochondria.

Organic sickness

In the case of physical (i.e. organic) illnesses, the person fears having a disease, and this is later confirmed by tests and exams. If this is the case, then the patient is experiencing the illness and not just imagining it. It is essentially normal. It isn't a fantasy however it is real.

Be afraid of the future

The fear of progress (FOP) is a worry that people feel in relation to the progress of a specific illness with all the negative consequences. What differentiates FOP from hypochondria is the fact that the physical illness is present and is present at an early stage or just mildly felt. It is commonly encountered by people who suffer from chronic illnesses and those who are concerned about the progression of signs.

Common Comorbidities (accompanying illness)

The difference between illnesses isn't always easy as hypochondrias are often associated with other illnesses. The primary disease must be identified before taking care of the other issues. On the next pages I'll briefly describe the most common accompanying diseases caused by hypochondria

Depression

Depression is one of the most frequent condition that is associated with hypochondria. Around 40 to half of hypochondriacs have depression in addition to. But, in most cases, the hypochondria is formed prior to depression this leads us to think that those with hypochondria are at the highest chance of being depressed.

Anxiety Disorders

The most frequent accompanying disease is anxiety especially panic attacks accompanied by Claustrophobia. They account for approximately a third associated illnesses. The anxiety disorders typically manifest simultaneously or just before hypochondria. Hypochondria may result after an anxiety attack and could be a parallel manifestation to it.

Somatoform diseases

While somatoform diseases are seen quite often, there's not much details on them as hypochondria has been regarded as an inferior form of Somatoform disorder. In the preceding pages, I've counted the somatoform condition as a distinct condition from hypochondria. The research suggests that between 7 and 21% of hypochondriacs also suffer from somatoform disorders.

Chapter 12: Hypochondria-related effects

The hypochondriacal condition has a significant impact on us and our community. Most of the time, we don't suffer on our own, but close family members and friends typically suffer as well.

Personal items

Hypochondria affects individuals. If you once were a happy and lively individual, it is possible that you're now sad, unhappy and go about your day, distracted by your thoughts.

People you work with observe that you're working more than usual while at work they notice that you're not attentive. The thought of being lost takes up a large portion of your time, and frequently hinders your focus on the work you are doing.

In your personal day life, your hypochondria affecting your leisure activities and interests. In particular, sports activities are ignored because you are trying to safeguard your body in which you feel sick.

Physical physical

It is a common cause of psychological signs however it could cause physical pain and issues. Stress, for instance, can result in you breaking out in sweats, feel heart anxiety, and even panic attacks.

In most cases, numerous drugs are used, and aren't necessary since there's no illness underlying. They can have adverse effects and may cause damage to the organs.

Impact on society

The most prominent result of hypochondria can be observed in its social effects. The focus is so on your own thoughts and fears that you become absorbed in your thoughts and worries that you are less connected to the people you have in your circle.

It could also result in you avoiding those who are closest to you. It can be the case when you don't feel that others care about you when you talk about your physical ailments or issues that bother you. There is no feeling like you're being considered serious and therefore you keep away from individuals.

Social isolation becomes more severe as you age and are being affected by hypochondria. It increases the risk of sinking deeper into your personal world and depressions emerge from the loneliness.

Chapter 13: Treatment for hypochondria

The treatment for every hypochondriac is different. The treatment for light or non-chronic conditions on your own. Particularly if symptoms or fears are not in the past six months, there's an excellent chance that you will be able to return to health. See the following section on this topic.

If the issues have been present for longer than half of an year, and doctors or psychotherapists fail to provide you with a sense of security and like your life is limited, it could indicate you're in need of professional assistance.

Traumatic, unprocessed or dramatic incidents can trigger the formation of hypochondria. Expert support may be required for you to get through these experiences.

The therapy program for professionals who treat hypochondria is mostly based around psychotherapy. Cognitive behavioural therapy appears to be the most popular. Psychotherapy in this form is used in addition to anxiety-related issues. The most challenging hypochondria cases are dealt with through medications.

Since the risk of comorbidity with depression panic attacks, anxiety as well as compulsive and somatisation disorders is quite high, additional disorders must be taken care of at the at the same time.

Psychotherapy for cognitive behavioural issues

In the case of anxiety disorders, cognitive behavioral therapy is the most commonly used method of treatment. The goal of this therapy is to one degree to alter the way that you think (cognitive) and to the contrary it is to alter behavior.

For the cognitive aspect of the process, it is important to diminish the false assumption, by the of the customer the belief that illness may be possible. Behaviors, like continuous monitoring of symptoms as well as regular visits to a doctor, must be altered.

The main goal of therapy is showing clients that certain bodily functions and feelings are completely normal, that are present in all people and not something to be concerned about. For instance the heartbeat, sweating, or even bowel movements.

Furthermore, the patient gets to know what physical manifestations such as stress or fear could cause to the body. Symptoms can be incorrectly understood.

Then there are additional experiments which you can carry out in order to determine what your body's reaction is to having numerous cups of coffee like, for instance, or sleeping deprivation. Additionally, you'll be taught how to assess the truthfully whether or not you're suffering from serious illness.

Then, you will receive a series of behaviour-based exercises to help you discover ways to alter your behavior. There are a variety of techniques to be employed in this regard, including the paradox of intensification of behavior as well as the creation reports, the reduction of the number of doctor appointments and your self-assurance strategies that you typically use, like talking with relatives or reading the news.

Psychotherapy

By undergoing psychotherapy, you'll be able to trust your body better and lessen the anxiety. Based on research Cognitive behavioural therapy in conjunction with confrontational therapy - where the client is required to confront their fears to get control of them, offers the greatest chance for being successful. For hypochondriacs this treatment is usually carried out within psychosomatic centers who are specially trained in treating anxiety disorders.

Psycho-sensory procedures

Psycho-sensory therapies are employed more and more successfully in treatment of anxiety and the anxiety of illness. The patient is taken into a world filled with color, light, music and warmth. It leads to greater relaxation, as well as feelings of peace and peace. The most well-known psycho-sensory methods include EMDR of Dr. Francine Shapiro, TFT by Dr. Roger Callahan, EFT from Gary Craig, OEI from Dr. Rick Bradshaw and colleagues Then there is 'Havening', which comes from the Dr. Ronald A. Ruden. It is not my intention to get too involved in the different psycho-sensory methods within this book. If you're interested in this area, I'd recommend reading some of the scientific literature and available for purchase.

The use of medicine

There is a lack of research on the efficacy of medical treatments for hypochondria. One of the most popular medications used is one that is frequently used to treat different psychiatric issues, such as known as selective serotonin reuptake inhibitor (SSRI).

Serotonin is one of the most important neurotransmitters within the brain. Its goal is to alleviate the symptoms associated with hypochondria with the help of SSRIs. But, there haven't so far any studies showing that the improvement in symptoms is stable even after patients quit taking the drug.

The condition is usually associated with other conditions. If you have a hypochondria that is accompanied by depression, anti-depressants can help.

If there is a severe case of schizophrenia, like hypochondriacal delusion or nerve stimulation, treatments - also known as neuroleptics - can be prescribed.

Progression and prognosis for hypochondria

Hypochondriacal disease is thought to be incurable. However when treated promptly through either professional assistance or self-help it is possible of restoring the health you enjoy are very high.

Stress from psychosocial factors, illnesses among friends or family members, or even life-changing events may trigger hypochondria. Relapses and even relapses could be a. It is crucial, however to recognize the fact that it's only stress that causes symptoms and is not actually an disease.

If through cognitive-behavioral therapy or self-help, are able to steer your thoughts away from the fear, then you are able to start using these methods for the second time.

It is crucial, for any disorder that is associated with it like depression or anxiety, are addressed at the same time, as hypochondria to get the most effective therapy results.

Chapter 14: Let go of your worries by completing four phases

Hypochondria can be cured however it will require time when you're doing your best to take care of yourself. Your own self is the only key to success. You just must learn what steps you can do for a life that is relaxed yet again.

I'll show you the steps by step the process I used to get rid of my hypochondriacal disorders. Nowadays, I'm feeling great and would love to share that with those who read this by sharing my self-developed idea, that gave me the life I wanted back.

This method has helped me, and I'm sure others can gain from it. Be aware that If you're not succeeding at overcoming your issues regardless of trying everything that you could, I would suggest insistently that you locate experts to assist you.

It is not possible to guarantee immediate healing. I'm trying to provide you with a method in a step-by-step manner the best way to deal with your own fears and anxieties to lessen them. There is no 100% guarantee that you will succeed, but I would like to encourage you to consider giving this a shot. You have absolutely nothing to lose, and a lot to gain.

Step 1: Observation

In the beginning take note of your habits over the following 7 days. The first thing to consider is the frequency you spend time by your body.

When I wrote down my observations I realized that I spent much of my time obsessed with my body. The time I could have been more productive when I was free from these anxieties.

Diary

Make a notepad and journal for 7 days. Record each moment you experience a sign or a fear. Each time you are thinking about illness or symptoms, take your thoughts down, including the date and time it occurred. Also note the amount of period you're online or in textbooks, looking up the symptoms you are experiencing. Keep track of the amount of time you spend on your research.

Based on my experiences I've seen this turn into an extensive list, but it doesn't matter. The contrary is that the longer your list is, faster you'll be able to see how far this differs from what is normal and the extent to which you would like to alter this.

Step 2: Insight

Based on your observations have you noticed your thinking and behavior consume a large portion of the day? If so,

I'm sure you're prepared for the next the most crucial action.

The next step isn't just the most crucial but it's equally difficult. If you've held the idea that you are suffering from an disease for an extended period of time It isn't easy to let go of the belief and realize that you're not sick.

Consultation with a doctor

It can assist you to determine for certain that you're healthy by seeing the doctor in your family. Talk to him about your feelings and the action can feel as. Maybe you require a second testing or blood test to allow you to believe that the illness you're experiencing is not real. It's fine so long as you are doing this in the hopes to prove to yourself that you are healthy. This is not a good idea to more anxiety and fear.

Visits to the doctor can also be beneficial to ensure you have a professional there to support you while seeking to get better. regular visits to the doctor, scheduled beforehand, and to check the progress you have made, could prove beneficial. The doctor will be more likely to recognize when you've lost your way or surrendering to the anxiety and letting your fears get the better of you.

Diagnostic results in white and black

You may be able by having a printed copy of the outcomes from your blood tests, as well as other outcomes, and there are likely to be many from the previous. It is your right to request all of your test outcomes.

Check out the findings both in black and white likely written by different doctors. It helped me realize my suspicions that the diagnosis were not established and the condition was not present.

Contact your relatives

Contact your closest relatives. This can help you discuss the reasons that led you to feel this manner, and also listen to their thoughts about you.

It was vital for me to involve my most trusted friends during the process. They were also experiencing some form of pain during my time of believing myself to be ill. The desperation of my wife didn't go without being noticed.

My loved ones were pleased having gained knowledge about my situation and that I could involve them in helping me in the course of. They became more close as we pursued the same goal. My relations with my family was sometimes difficult in the hypochondriacal stages due to the fact that they didn't feel like me and didn't take my illness as seriously. Perhaps you've experienced this you have. It is the reason I am here for you to reach out with your most trusted friends. Join them as you travel and battle your anxieties with them. With this community to your side, you will have the support you need in the process of releasing your body from hypochondriacal disorders.

Step 3. Mind control

You recorded your observations about the thoughts you had about illness and also your fear. The third step is managing and controlling the anxiety that arises.

Be able to stop worrying and having thoughts concerning your body. Say "Stop" to yourself and refrain from allowing your thoughts to persist. By saying "stop", you should put off your online search or plan to go to your doctor.

Positive affirmation

Positive affirmations are a powerful strategy to fight anxiety and fears. It can help you manage your thoughts and processes, as well as change or improve the way you think about them.

Affirmations are simple positive, affirmative statements which can help you reach your goals. They are useful throughout the day in any situation. They can be used to break out of our thought habits.

It seems like a straightforward task initially. The trick is to form sentences, that seem to make sense to you. The answer is based on how you feel and think. The ability to summarize that in one word will alter your mind as well as your thinking processes over the long run.

Make a positive affirmation written on the back of a Post-it or on a piece of paper. Be sure to avoid negative words in your phrase like "not" or "none" for instance, as these words are subconsciously removed of your brain, and your sentence could have an opposite impact. For instance, the sentence "I am not afraid". It is better to write it in a way that it says "I am free from anxiety, fearless and self-confident".

These are the sentences which I came up with and applied. They are intended to serve as an example. It's better to come up with your own sentences that you will be able to speak in a confident manner:

"I am feeling better and better about my body, every day."

"My body is healthy and resilient."

"I am feeling a little bit better every day."

"I love the feeling of being able to make decisions about my own life."

There must be the feeling of each affirmation. It is important to feel a sense of connection with them in order to ensure that you don't just speak the words, but they are able to reach your unconscious.

There is no one who was born to be to be a master. The practice of positive affirmations took some time to master. It is recommended to stand before an mirror and gazing in your own eyes as you speak the phrases. Make sure you speak in your own voice! This might seem odd at first, so it could take time until you're at ease with this method.

There are many ways to make use of affirmations. Examples:

Then, you say them out loud at your mirror, and then gaze into the mirror.

They come to mind when you think of them.

Then you say them loudly in your head.

They are repeated every whenever you rise or fall asleep.

Write them down again each day.

Then, you write your thoughts on Post-it notes or on a piece of paper, and then hang the posters around your house.

Sing them out to yourself.

It is easy to let them show up every day on your schedule, smartphone or computer.

Then, you play them using a pre-recorded recording of audio which is a type of message recorded.

The sentences that I made helped me in one way to improve my mental clarity as well as, on the other on the other hand, I utilized to help me cope to help me cope with an illness for instance, a headache. In these instances I spoke my sentences in my head or loudly, depending upon the circumstances:

"I am feeling better and better about my body, every day. My body is healthy and resilient. I am feeling a little bit better every day. I love the feeling of being able to make decisions about my own life."

By using affirmations, I am able to drive off negativity of my thoughts prior to when they get controlling me. I'm declaring "stop" to the negative thoughts that I was accustomed to and steering myself to positive thinking.

The words I read each day, no matter in times of good health I carry them on my lips and help make me stronger.

Step 4: Stabilisation

The 4th step is where you're now able to regulate your thoughts as well as get rid of negative thoughts. You can tell when you are in danger, this may lead you back to those old thoughts. The affirmations you make help overcome them and to maintain the convictions you have.

You're on the right track! Repeat that mantra to yourself over and over and over and again. Remind yourself of your affirmations. At this point, it's enough to think about it at least once per daily. Important is that you have a feeling of a connection to these sentences.

At this point you must achieve stability and calm for your body, so that you are sturdy and avoid falling back to your old routines. Physical activities or sports will help with this as well as relaxing techniques. I'll be presenting various ways to relax in the next section.

Physical activity and sports

Most people do not realize the significance of sports and other exercise. Being a hypochondriac you are likely to become overprotective toward your body because you are afraid of falling ill. This means that the stamina of your body gets worse and leads the body to experience greater physical discomfort, as a result due to your condition being poor.

Begin your exercise or activity today and then incorporate your routine in order to increase your energy. Be careful not to do it too much. One of the best ways to do this is to start slow but remain focussed. Do some type of exercise each daily. Choose the type of exercise you are most interested in. Do you like ball sports? Do you enjoy dancing? Are you interested in dancing? Zumba an option that is suitable for you? There are a myriad of options to get active. It is essential, however finding what you are interested in doing.

I am a lover of nature, and began to bicycle at least 3 to four times per week regardless of weather conditions. It started out with shorter distances, but over time I've noticed that my endurance has increased, permitting me to travel greater distances. It helps me believe in myself and feel fit and energized. Sometimes, it allows me manage anxiety by repeating affirmations each time I press the brake until my mind is clear.

To enhance my fitness and muscle strength to strengthen my muscles, I practice exercise at home to strengthen my muscles, by using my body. This is called bodyweight training. I purchased some fitness DVDs specifically to help me with this. I don't like being in fitness facilities in a large way, so I chose to search for a fitness program that I could perform at my own pace, no matter where I happen to be.

There are many options. In the beginning, you'll need lots of discipline in order to get over your insecure self however, once the fitness becomes the norm of your life and you begin to notice that you'll never desire to go without it, as it feels so more relaxed and healthier.

Meditation and yoga

Yoga is an old Indian philosophy that is about the union of mind, body and spirit at the core. People who practice yoga across the globe generally perform the physical exercise (Asanas) as well as breathing practices (Pranayama). The primary goal of yoga is "liberating redemption".

The primary distinction between yoga and regular exercise is that it maintains the posture of your body and an emphasis on breathing. There's always a link between the technique of breathing and the concentration on the inner self. The exercise forms contain particular instructions are provided when you breathe in and out. Heartbeats speed up as you breathe in, and breath out causes your pulse to slow. This is the way you influence the nervous system as well as regulate your organs and muscles.

Yoga improves metabolic process and helps strengthen your nervous system. Additionally, breathing exercises can help reduce stress and tension.

Today meditation and yoga are often regarded as a way to maintain or improve well-being and to ease stress.

I find yoga to be the best way to regulate both mind and body. Its "sun salutation" has become an integral element of my daily routine and every day I begin my morning by doing it. In the days that I plan more physical activities I like to increase my time in yoga.

Begin with easy activities at first, particularly even if you've never had much experience in yoga or join an established yoga class near your house.

Relaxation techniques

As well as physical exercise and relaxation, I suggest learning some methods and applying them frequently. People with hypochondriac tend to live their life in a stressed as well as obsessive, and their minds do not let go of its tense state.

For a way to put a bit of separation from the negative thoughts that plague you, relaxing techniques such as an autogenic or progressive muscle training, may help.

Discover which method of relaxation you enjoy and practice it frequently. This can help you discover inner peace and, in the end, you'll feel more at harmony.

Chapter 15: Relaxation techniques and instruction

Our society's desire for balance in our lives is increasing. The desire for calm in our working and daily life. Many people are engaging in relaxation methods and techniques that aren't only helpful in helping to treat ailments and therapies, but also are advised for all to use.

Four methods that I have found to be extremely effective for to relax and release stress, anxiety and anxieties are: Progressive relaxation of muscles as well as autogenic exercise Yoga and meditation.

Here I'll introduce you to two techniques of relaxation that are progressive muscle relaxation as well as autogenic exercise - as I believe they're less popular than such things as yoga.

Progressive Muscle Relaxation

The concept of progressive muscle relaxation also known as PMR in short PMR was invented during the 1920s, in particular in the early 1920s by American psychotherapist Edmund Jacobson. It's often referred to as PMR as per Jacobson. Jacobson was searching for exercises to ease his back pain that had resulted from sitting for a long time at a desk. As he performed his relaxing exercise, he realized that it wasn't just the muscles that relaxed and relaxed, but his thoughts also improved. He believed that the muscle tension is always linked to tension or excitement. In in another way anxiety, stress, and emotional stress may also be lessened by decreasing the tension in muscles.

The method is easy to master and therefore appropriate for everyone. It doesn't require any specific equipment or a program of instruction. It can be practiced practically anyplace.

In the event of specific situations or incidents that create stress such as before an exam or flight. It is possible to do short sections of PMR not being spotted and thus you'll be able to quickly get relaxation from tension or stress.

Aim

The primary goal of this technique is to build a "muscular sense" by training your body for greater awareness of yourself.

Another focus is the diminution of anxiety. PMR can reduce tension and anxiety. Regularly performing the exercises can result in less psychological symptoms associated with tension like tension, tremors and headaches or heart palpitations.

Applications

PMR is usually employed in conjunction with behavioural therapy. It's proven to be very effective for treating anxiety and borderline disorder. Also, it is an effective companion treatment to headaches, high blood pressure and chronic backaches, sleep problems and anxiety.

Contraindications

PMR isn't recommended to treat schizophrenia or those who suffer from obsessional tendencies. When this happens the treatment could be detrimental to the patient. It is generally not recommended for hypochondria since it forces the patient to focus more intensely at his body.

I would recommend PMR for hypochondria mainly in the 4th stage, the stage of stabilisation.

Two aspects of PMR

Physical aspect:

The major muscle groups are stretched out, with instructions, for 5 to 7 seconds per and in a specific sequence. Tension is removed and the user can feel the impact of relaxation.

Your eyes are closed during the workout, ensuring that there is no distraction from the visual. In this way, you are able to focus on your personal awareness and notice the distinction between relaxation and tension.

In the end, the sensation of easing muscle tension is vital. Relaxation that happens can be felt directly in the body. In contrast to a calm mind, in these conditions relaxing the body can be felt in the muscles.

The more enthusiastic you feel when you begin and the higher your risk of straining your muscles to the point of overuse. It can cause muscles stiffness or cramps the following day. It is therefore suggested that you stretch the muscle to about 80% of your maximal. This is about the threshold, but you should not push it beyond the limit.

The psychological aspect of PMR:

The mental aspect of PMR is different from the physical one in that it doesn't focus on tension or relaxation of muscles. The focus is on feeling how different they are.

The most advanced practitioners of PMR are not required to do physical training, they may do it mentally, similar to training that is autogenic, which is that is based on the ability to listen the body. People imagine how their muscles relax so that muscles can be relaxed. The most experienced people are able to reach the state of complete relaxation within a short period of time using this strategy.

The mental aspect of this exercise requires lots of practice as well as years of experience in PMR. Still learning. My current level of proficiency is not proficient with my mental practice. I am able to feel the power and relaxation far more when using the physical body, however that doesn't mean that I'll never have the ability to utilize the mental model efficiently in the future.

Instructions

Duration:

It will take you between 15-30 minutes to complete the exercise.

Preparation:

Find a peaceful place in which you won't be disturbed. The best way to do this is to perform the practice lying or sitting down.

If it is possible you can dim the lights just slightly.

Lay on your back, Relax and lay back. It is possible to lay your head on a blanket if would like. Place 2 or 3 cushions beneath the knee joint If you require these.

Set your legs further apart, with your arms a ways from your body. Keep your with your palms facing up, and shoulder distance from your ears, and then stretch your neck out.

Implementation:

Then we'll focus on body components through the next five steps:

The first step is to locate the part of your body that needs to be repaired,

To tighten muscles, you must exercise the part of your body that is tight,

Keep the tension in place,

Let the tension release slowly.

Relax the muscles.

Arms and hands

Take note of the right hand. Relax the hand on the right side and the forearm. Slowly, form in a fist. Tense the forearm. Form a powerful fist. Feel the muscle tension. Hold the tension and observe how your forearm and the right hand are feeling. Then slowly let the tension go and relax the fingers and forearms.

The left hand should be felt. Relax the left hand. the forearm. Gradually make an elongated fist, and then tense the forearm. Form a powerful fist, and feel the muscle tension. Hold the tension for a moment, note how tension on the left hand and forearm feel. Slowly release the tension and feel the relief within the forearm and fingers.

Be aware of the right hand, starting with the fingers and ending at the shoulder. Tensify your entire arm. Repeat the fist, then place the arm on the ground. Feel the tension on the arm. Keep the tension in your mind and observe what it feels like, gradually letting the arm relax. Relax the arm muscles.

Take note of the left arm starting with the fingers, all the way towards the shoulder. Tense your entire arm. Repeat the fist, then push the arm towards the ground. Feel the tension on the arm. Take note of the tension and what it feels like, gradually letting the arm relax. You will feel the relief in your muscles of the arm.

Head and face:

Be aware of your face, starting from your chin, all the way to your forehead all the way until the top of your head. The face muscles are tense through contracting all muscles that reach the tip of your nose. Include your eyebrows. Then, furrow the forehead and brows. tighten your cheek muscles until the point the tip of your nose. Begin to feel the tension and slowly let it go by feeling the relaxedness of your face muscles.

The neck and throat are felt. Bring your chin towards your chest and push the head's back lightly into the floor or cushions. Notice the tension that is present in your neck. Release it slowly and feel the relief within the muscles of your neck.

Torso:

Take note of your back and torso from the buttocks and lower back, to the mid back and the upper back. Bring your shoulder blades closer as you tighten the muscles of your stomach and buttocks. Be aware of the tension that is in your body and then hold to it. The tension will be felt, and then gradually let it go. You will feel the relief in your muscles in your torso.

Feet and legs:

The right leg should be felt all the way from your toes from your calves, to your legs. Bring your toes up towards your head, and then raise the tension on your leg. Place your heels on the ground and tighten the muscles on the leg on your right. Notice the tension and gently ease it. Relax the muscles on the right leg.

The left leg should be felt beginning at the toes and extending down your calves and into your legs. Move your feet upwards toward your head, and then raise the tension on your leg. Put your heels in the floor, and tense muscles in your left leg. Be aware of the tension on the left leg and slowly let it go. You will feel the relaxed muscles in the left leg.

Relax and enjoy this sensation of calm throughout your body. You will feel the same relaxation in every muscle group, each one at a moment beginning with your feet and moving to your head muscles. head. Relax and feel calm for a couple of minutes without interruption.

It is here that we start with closing the exercise and begin to unwind. Then, you are able to use affirmations, like "I feel wide awake, peaceful and refreshed". That's something you are able to say at this point with conviction as you complete the exercise.

Training with autogenics

Autogenic training is a relaxing method that relies on auto-suggestion. The psychologist Johannes Heinrich Schultz from Berlin came up with the idea out of the hypnosis practice and introduced it for the first time in 1926. Schultz's relaxation technique is modified method of hypnosis that relies on the use of a person's imagination in order to attain a state calm, but not achieving the massive changes in consciousness like in hypnosis. The man once referred to his technique of self-hypnosis in the form of "Yoga of the west".

As opposed to yoga and other kinds of meditations it is not a practice that deals in a state of relaxation and tension, and in reality, it's entirely devoid of any physical activities. Instead, you focus on simple auto-suggestive exercise that result in being in a state of deep relaxation.

Through the practice of autogenic training, you will be able to attain a state that is a state of relaxation. This are able to significantly influence your mental and physical state. As an example, it could result in the end of compulsive behaviors or lessen stress and allow you to control your work daily.

Anybody can master autogenic training. It's up to you which method you would prefer. by using a professional trainer such as a DVD or video, or if you prefer to learn all by yourself. It is possible to find a vast assortment of video clips in which you can get an autogenic education through step-by-step. Test it. It is impossible to do it wrong.

Aim

It's a holistic approach which aims at restoring the balance between the body, mind and soul. The goal of this method is to concentrate your mind to achieve the physical and mental peace and calm.

When you are in autogenic training, it is important that the focus should be only on you and keep your focus on yourself. It is important to be in what is "here and now" and avoid allowing you to get distracted by external distractions.

Applications

Training with autogenics can allow almost everyone to live a better enjoyment in life as well as better well-being. As an example, physical training can be beneficial for getting better results whether at work or during sport as well as to improve your sleep or learn.

The autogenic method of training is extremely beneficial in fighting dependence issues, like alcohol, smoking or other addiction-causing substances.

In most cases, autogenic instruction is utilized to aid self-help, that can be utilized in a myriad of situations. It can be reassuring in dealing with a wide variety of illnesses. A few examples are laid out in the following table:

Hypertension

Sleep disorders

For example, migraines, headaches, chronic discomfort

Tinnitus

Irritable bowel syndrome

Metabolic diseases

Bronchial asthma

Libido disorders

Eating disorders, such as overweight or underweight

Cardio-vascular disorders

Nervous irritability

Insecurity

Agitation

Anxiety is a state of mind.

Depression

Complexes of inferiority

Nerves of the exam

Troubles in concentration

Contraindications

It is not suggested because of problems with the nervous system central, or mental impairment.

For psychosis, such as hypochondria it is recommended to talk with your therapist before beginning autogenic exercises.

As with the progressive relaxation of muscles I would recommend training with autogenous only during Step 4, which is the time of stabilisation.

Three fundamental steps to autogenic training

Training for autogenics is split into three phases. This first stage is appropriate for novices and necessary to get started on the following step. The next steps increase in intensity.

The Basic Step:

The methods in the initial section are geared towards the nervous system of the vegetative, certain muscles and the entire cardiovascular system. This is the complete routine for physical relaxation that is especially suitable for those who are new to the sport. In the near future, I'll discuss more in depth regarding this.

The Intermediate Step:

This is a stage for advanced learners. The goal is to empower those exercises that were learnt in the initial stage, by using your personal (or the provided) formulas. This part focuses specifically on the social and emotional aspects since it has to do the changes in behavior or attitudes.

The Advanced Step:

This is the step for people who have focused intensely on autogenic learning and have completed the steps 1 and 2. The techniques, utilized in the step of advanced focus on individual experiences or self-discovery. Through the use of formulistic resolution, it's possible to go further into the subconscious. This could trigger outbursts of feelings or events that had not been surfacing up until the point at which they appeared.